AF575018

ALSO BY **GRADY KLEIN** AND **YORAM BAUMAN, Ph.D.**

VOLUME ONE: MICROECONOMICS

THE CARTOON INTRODUCTION TO ECONOMICS

VOLUME TWO: MACROECONOMICS

THE CARTOON INTRODUCTION TO ECONOMICS

VOLUME TWO: MACROECONOMICS

BY **GRADY KLEIN** AND

YORAM BAUMAN, Ph.D.

THE WORLD'S FIRST AND ONLY **STAND-UP ECONOMIST**

A NOVEL GRAPHIC FROM HILL AND WANG

A DIVISION OF FARRAR, STRAUS AND GIROUX

NEW YORK

HILL AND WANG
A DIVISION OF FARRAR, STRAUS AND GIROUX
18 WEST 18TH STREET, NEW YORK 10011

DISTRIBUTED IN CANADA BY D&M PUBLISHERS, INC.
PRINTED IN THE UNITED STATES OF AMERICA
FIRST EDITION, 2012

LIBRARY OF CONGRESS CATALOGING-IN-PUBLICATION DATA

KLEIN, GRADY.
THE CARTOON INTRODUCTION TO ECONOMICS / BY GRADY KLEIN AND YORAM BAUMAN. — 1ST ED.
V. ; CM.
CONTENTS: VOL. 1. MICROECONOMICS.
ISBN: 978-0-8090-9481-3 (PBK. : ALK. PAPER)
1. MICROECONOMICS. I. BAUMAN, YORAM. II. TITLE.

HB172. K67 2009
338.5-DC22

2009015727

VOLUME TWO ISBN: 978-0-8090-3361-4

WWW.FSGBOOKS.COM

3 5 7 9 10 8 6 4 2

FOR ANNE AND LIAM AND BENJAMIN
—GK

FOR LAURA
—YB

CONTENTS

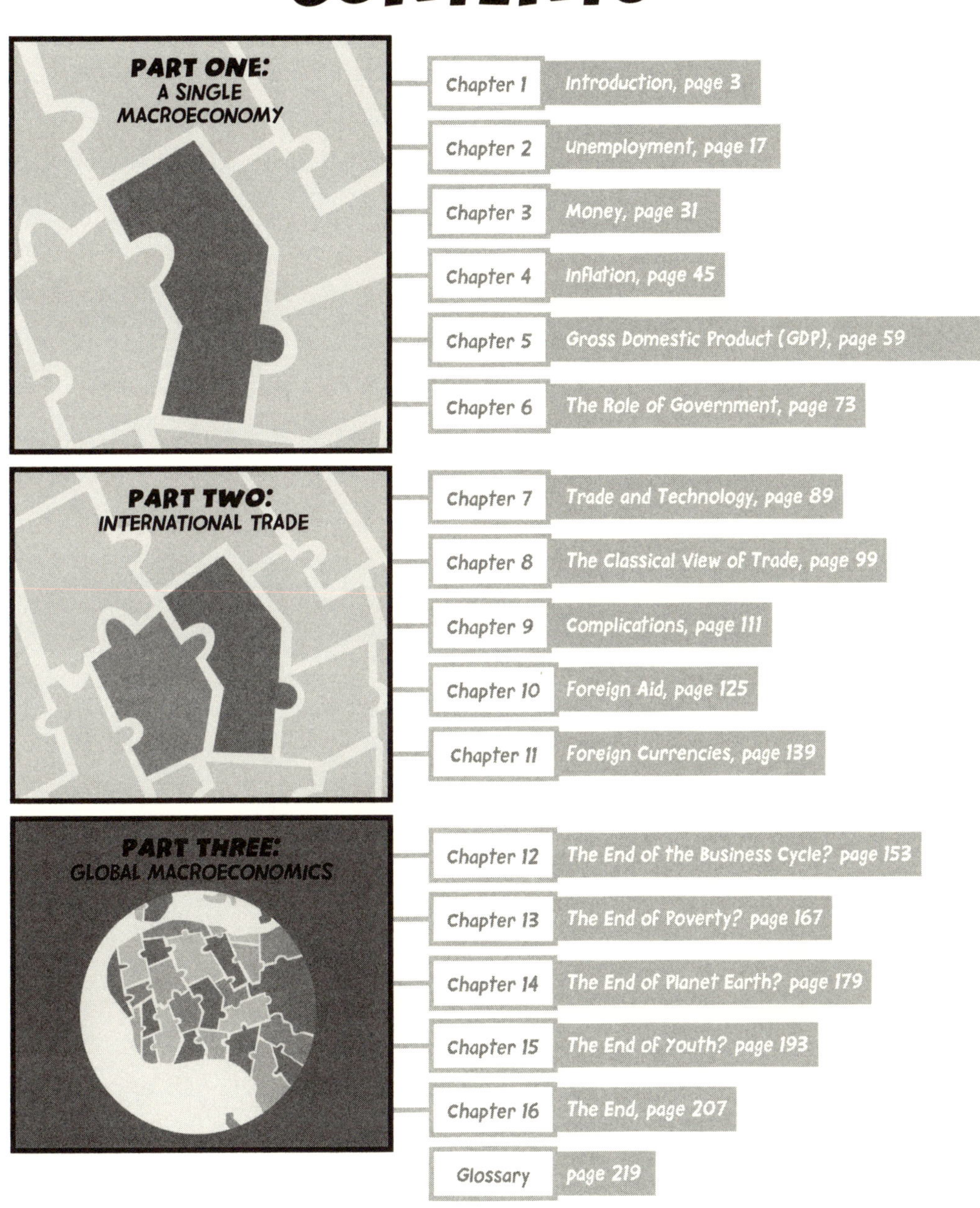

PART ONE
A SINGLE MACROECONOMY

CHAPTER 1
INTRODUCTION

OUR PREVIOUS BOOK WAS ABOUT **MICROECONOMICS**...

...WHICH LOOKS AT **THE ACTIONS AND INTERACTIONS** OF OPTIMIZING INDIVIDUALS.

THIS BOOK IS ABOUT
MACROECONOMICS...

...WHICH LOOKS AT ISSUES THAT AFFECT
THE ECONOMY OF AN ENTIRE COUNTRY...

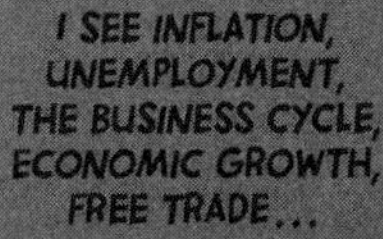

...OR EVEN THE **ENTIRE PLANET**.

THE **MACROECONOMY OF A COUNTRY** INCLUDES **ALL** THE DIFFERENT INDIVIDUAL MARKETS WE STUDIED IN MICROECONOMICS...

...SO **EVERYTHING** WE LEARNED ABOUT MICROECONOMICS...

...**STILL APPLIES HERE!**

... MACROECONOMISTS **DON'T** JUMP TO THE CONCLUSION THAT **PEOPLE ARE CRAZY OR STUPID.**

INSTEAD, MACROECONOMISTS STRIVE TO UNDERSTAND HOW PEOPLE CAN BE **OPTIMIZING**...

AND OF COURSE WHEN THINGS ARE **GOING WELL**, ECONOMISTS USE OPTIMIZING INDIVIDUALS TO EXPLAIN THAT, TOO.

MACROECONOMICS HAS **TWO BIG GOALS.**

ONE IS TO **INCREASE LIVING STANDARDS IN THE LONG RUN,** SO THAT TODAY'S KIDS WILL BE BETTER OFF THAN THEIR GRANDPARENTS...

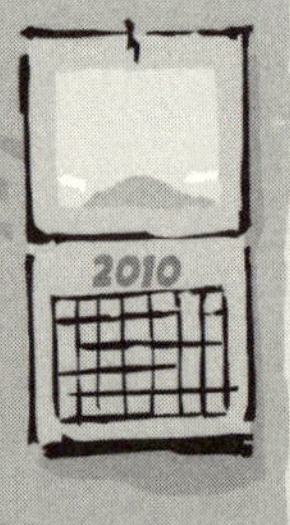

...JUST AS **THOSE GRANDPARENTS** WERE PROBABLY BETTER OFF THAN **THEIR** GRANDPARENTS...

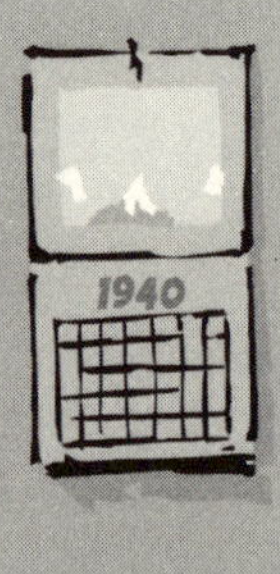

...AND SO ON.

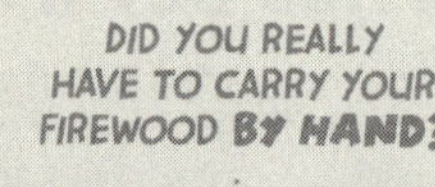

THE GOAL OF INCREASING LIVING STANDARDS GOES ALL THE WAY BACK TO **ADAM "INVISIBLE HAND" SMITH.**

IN 1776, ADAM SMITH INTRODUCED A **MACROECONOMICS METAPHOR**...

...THAT ECHOES TO THIS DAY.

THE IDEA THAT THE MACROECONOMY IS LIKE A WELL-ORGANIZED FAMILY IS CALLED **THE CLASSICAL VIEW**.

MOST ECONOMISTS AGREE THAT THE CLASSICAL VIEW MAKES A LOT OF SENSE **IN THE LONG RUN**.

THERE'S ONLY ONE **PROBLEM**:

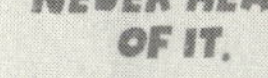

THIS LED THE BRITISH ECONOMIST **JOHN MAYNARD KEYNES** TO MAKE THE FIRST-EVER MACROECONOMICS JOKE:

"IN THE LONG RUN WE ARE ALL **DEAD.**"

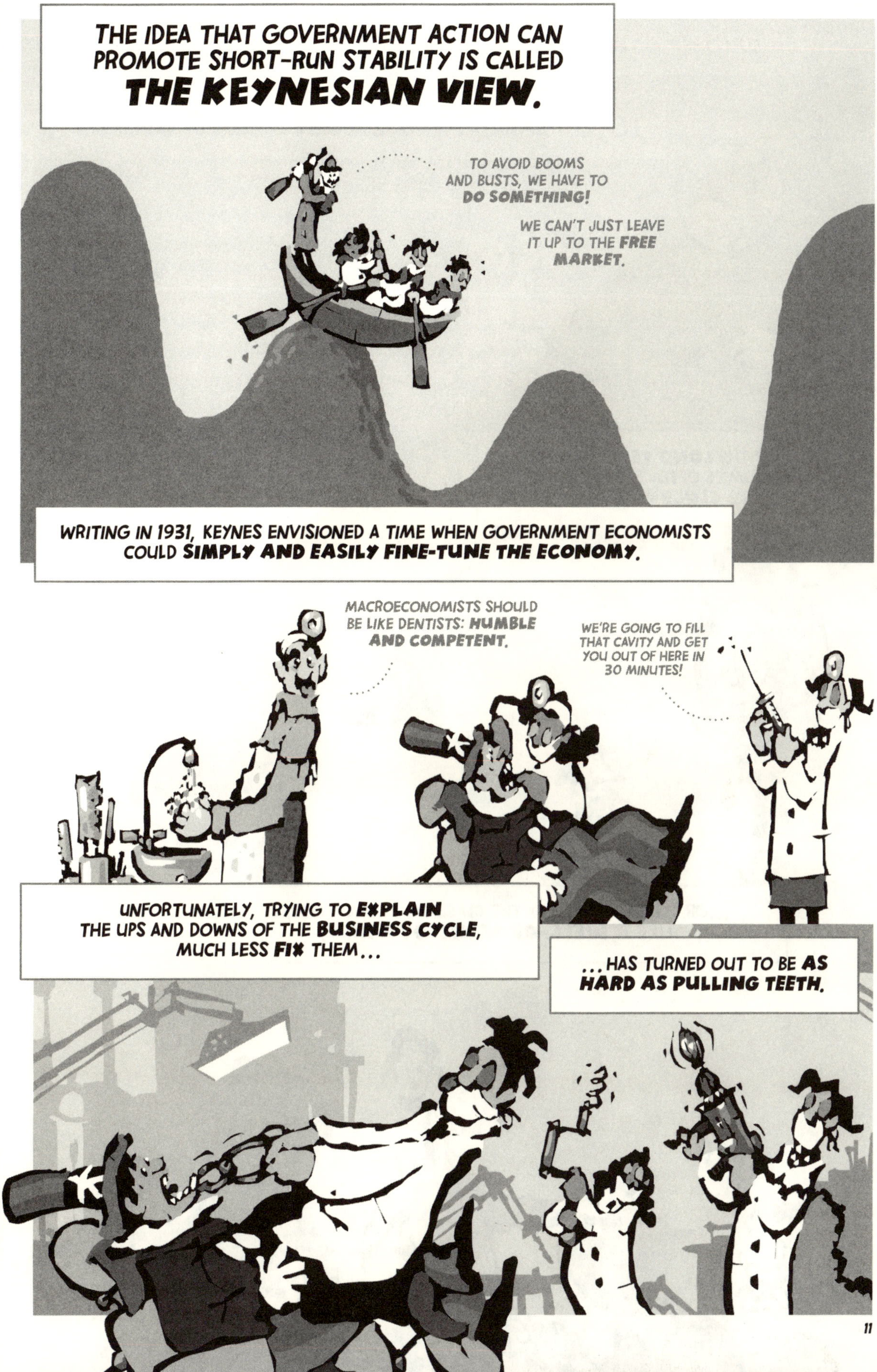

MACROECONOMISTS SHOULD BE LIKE DENTISTS: **HUMBLE AND COMPETENT.**

WE'RE GOING TO FILL THAT CAVITY AND GET YOU OUT OF HERE IN 30 MINUTES!

UNFORTUNATELY, TRYING TO **EXPLAIN** THE UPS AND DOWNS OF THE **BUSINESS CYCLE,** MUCH LESS **FIX** THEM...

...HAS TURNED OUT TO BE **AS HARD AS PULLING TEETH.**

IN SUM, THE **TWO BIG GOALS** OF MACROECONOMICS ARE:

TO EXPLAIN **HOW ECONOMIES GROW**...

400 YEARS AGO, ALMOST EVERYONE ON PLANET EARTH WAS **POOR**...

...400 YEARS FROM NOW, MAYBE EVERYONE WILL BE **RICH**!

OVER THE **LONG TERM**, ENTIRE ECONOMIES OFTEN SEEM TO RUN LIKE **CLOCKWORK**...

...OR LIKE **A RACEHORSE**...

...OR, AS SUGGESTED BY THE CLASSICAL ECONOMISTS, LIKE **A WELL-ORGANIZED FAMILY**.

ALL IS FOR THE BEST IN THIS, THE **BEST OF ALL POSSIBLE WORLDS**.

...AND WHY ECONOMIES COLLAPSE.
NEVER MIND ABOUT 400 YEARS...
...WHAT HAPPENED TO THE JOB I HAD YESTERDAY?
IN THE SHORT TERM, ENTIRE ECONOMIES SOMETIMES SEEM MORE LIKE A BUSTED CLOCK...
...OR LIKE A BUCKING BRONCO...
...OR, AS SUGGESTED BY THE KEYNESIAN ECONOMISTS, LIKE A DYSFUNCTIONAL FAMILY.

THIS BOOK LOOKS AT **MACROECONOMICS** BY STUDYING THE ECONOMY OF **ONE COUNTRY**...

THIS COUNTRY IS LIKE A GREAT BIG **HAPPY FAMILY!**
OH, PLEASE!

...AND THEN TRADE BETWEEN **TWO COUNTRIES**...

OR EVEN BETWEEN **TWO PLANETS.**

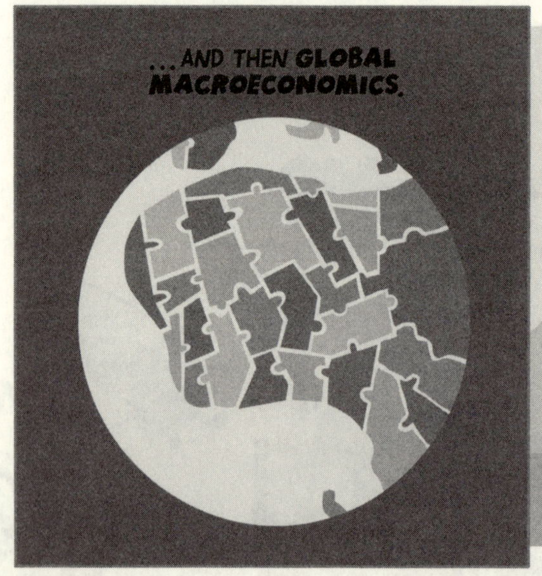
...AND THEN **GLOBAL MACROECONOMICS.**

HLWOO ZEELNOO FLOUDABLZ, **GHOW NEERP** GRSA!
ZANTROK SAYS WE HUMANS HAVE SOME BIG ISSUES TO DEAL WITH.

ALL ALONG, WE'LL BE FOLLOWING THE QUEST FOR **THE HOLY GRAIL** OF MACROECONOMICS:

HOW TO GET ECONOMIES TO GROW WITHOUT CRASHING.

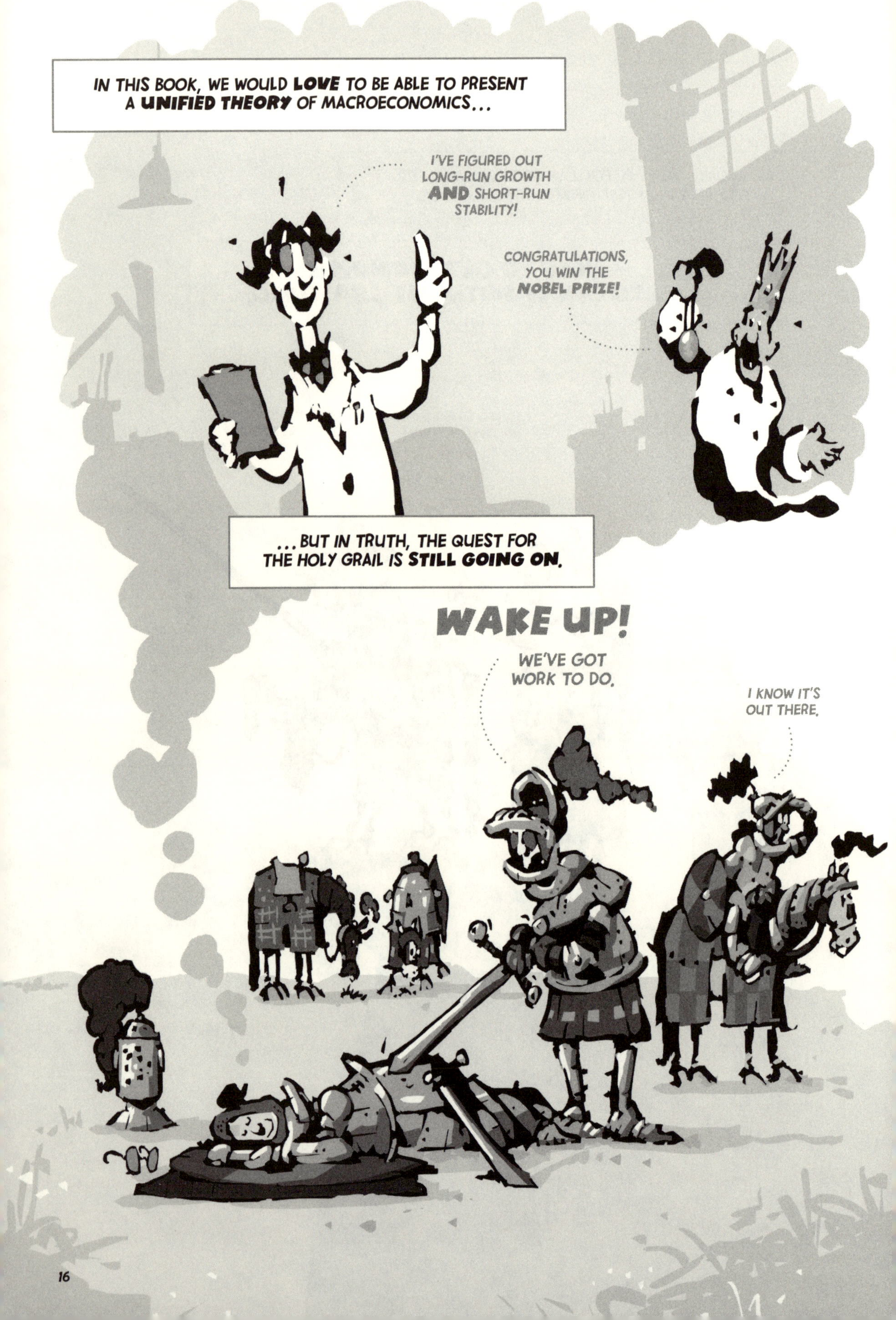

IN THIS BOOK, WE WOULD **LOVE** TO BE ABLE TO PRESENT A **UNIFIED THEORY** OF MACROECONOMICS...

...BUT IN TRUTH, THE QUEST FOR THE HOLY GRAIL IS **STILL GOING ON.**

WAKE UP!

WE'VE GOT WORK TO DO.

I KNOW IT'S OUT THERE.

CHAPTER 2
UNEMPLOYMENT

THE BEST WAY TO UNDERSTAND **THE KEYNESIAN VIEW OF THE ECONOMY...**

...IS TO LOOK AT THE **LABOR MARKET.**

IN THE SHORT RUN, MESSED-UP ECONOMIES CAN LEAVE **LOTS** OF PEOPLE OUT OF WORK.

DURING THE **GREAT DEPRESSION**, FOR EXAMPLE, THE UNEMPLOYMENT RATE PEAKED IN 1933 AT A SHOCKING **25%.**

MORE RECENTLY, THE "GREAT RECESSION" THAT STARTED IN DECEMBER 2007 FEATURED AN EXTENDED PERIOD OF **HIGH UNEMPLOYMENT**, PEAKING IN 2009 AT 10%.

BUT LOOKING AT THE **LABOR MARKET** IS **ALSO** THE BEST WAY TO UNDERSTAND...

...THE **CLASSICAL VIEW OF THE ECONOMY.**

IN THE LONG RUN, DESPITE **MASSIVE CHANGES** IN THE LABOR MARKET OVER THE PAST TWO CENTURIES...

LIKE POPULATION GROWTH...

THE ENTRY OF WOMEN INTO THE LABOR FORCE...

TECHNOLOGICAL CHANGE...

AND GLOBALIZATION...

...FREE-MARKET ECONOMIES HAVE CONTINUED TO CREATE JOBS FOR PRETTY MUCH **EVERYBODY.**

TO UNDERSTAND THE **CLASSICAL VIEW,** LET'S LOOK AT THE **U.S.** AND **EUROPE.**

UNTIL ABOUT 1800, THEIR JOB MARKETS WERE DOMINATED BY **AGRICULTURE.**

BY 1930, MOST OF THOSE JOBS WERE GONE, BUT THEY WERE REPLACED BY OTHER JOBS SUCH AS **MANUFACTURING.**

AND IN THE 21ST CENTURY, MANY OF THOSE JOBS ARE GOING AWAY AND BEING REPLACED BY **SERVICE-SECTOR JOBS.**

THE LESSON HERE IS THAT, OVER TIME, **WORK DISAPPEARS FROM SOME PARTS** OF A FREE-MARKET ECONOMY...

...BUT **REAPPEARS ELSEWHERE.**

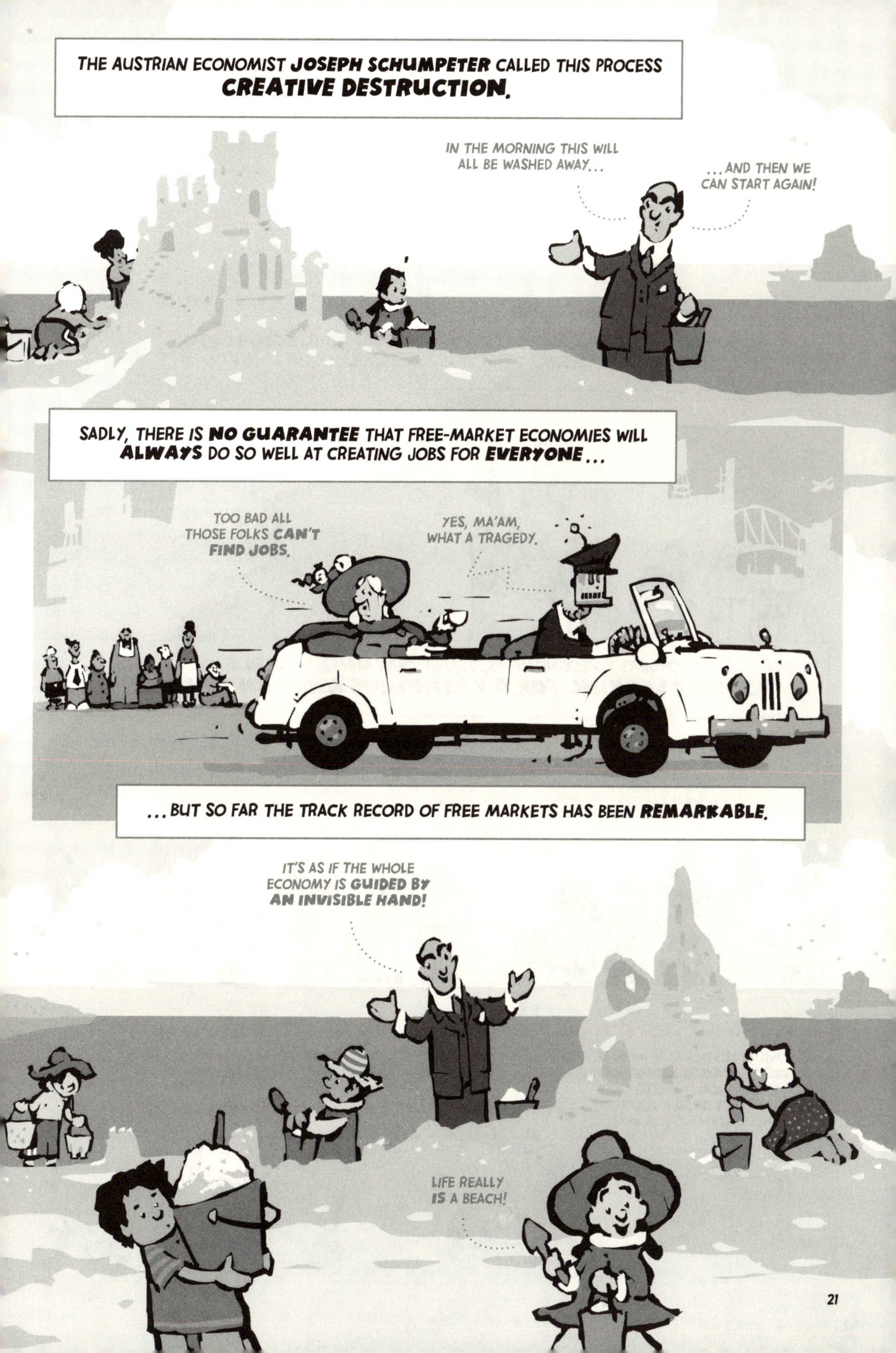

THE AUSTRIAN ECONOMIST **JOSEPH SCHUMPETER** CALLED THIS PROCESS **CREATIVE DESTRUCTION.**

SADLY, THERE IS **NO GUARANTEE** THAT FREE-MARKET ECONOMIES WILL **ALWAYS** DO SO WELL AT CREATING JOBS FOR **EVERYONE**...

...BUT SO FAR THE TRACK RECORD OF FREE MARKETS HAS BEEN **REMARKABLE.**

IT'S AS IF THE WHOLE ECONOMY IS **GUIDED BY AN INVISIBLE HAND!**

LIFE REALLY **IS** A BEACH!

WHEN IT COMES TO THE LABOR MARKET, THE CHALLENGE IS TO **RECONCILE THE CLASSICAL AND THE KEYNESIAN VIEWS.**

TO DO THIS, IT HELPS TO HAVE A GOOD **DEFINITION OF "UNEMPLOYMENT,"** A SIMPLE-SOUNDING TERM THAT IS ACTUALLY QUITE TRICKY.

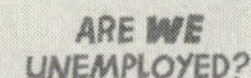

ACCORDING TO ECONOMISTS, YOU'RE ONLY **UNEMPLOYED** IF YOU'RE **ACTIVELY LOOKING FOR A PAYING JOB AND CAN'T FIND ONE.**

SOME STATISTICS ALSO INCLUDE **DISCOURAGED WORKERS**, BUT TECHNICALLY YOU'RE ONLY **UNEMPLOYED** IF YOU'RE ACTIVELY LOOKING FOR WORK.

ECONOMISTS ALSO DISTINGUISH BETWEEN **THREE BASIC TYPES** OF UNEMPLOYMENT.

FRICTIONAL

STRUCTURAL

CYCLICAL

THE FIRST TYPE, **FRICTIONAL UNEMPLOYMENT**, IS UNAVOIDABLE SHORT-TERM UNEMPLOYMENT CAUSED BY CHANGES IN THE ECONOMY AND IN PEOPLE'S LIVES.

FRICTIONAL UNEMPLOYMENT MAKES SENSE TO **BOTH** CLASSICAL AND KEYNESIAN ECONOMISTS.

TO UNDERSTAND THE **SECOND TYPE** OF UNEMPLOYMENT, RECALL FROM MICRO THAT THE **PRICE OF LABOR** IS SUPPOSED TO **BALANCE SUPPLY AND DEMAND.**

LONG-TERM UNEMPLOYMENT THAT RESULTS WHEN THIS PROCESS BREAKS DOWN IS CALLED **STRUCTURAL UNEMPLOYMENT.**

THE OBVIOUS QUESTION IS: **WHY DON'T WAGES FALL** TO BALANCE SUPPLY AND DEMAND?

ONE POSSIBLE CAUSE IS **MINIMUM WAGE LAWS.**

ANOTHER POSSIBILITY IS **EFFICIENCY WAGES.**

PARADOXICALLY, STRUCTURAL UNEMPLOYMENT CAN ALSO RESULT FROM GOVERNMENT POLICIES THAT ARE INTENDED TO **PRESERVE JOBS.**

THE PARADOX IS THAT FIRMS THAT CANNOT EASILY **FIRE** WORKERS ARE ALSO GOING TO BE SLOW TO **HIRE** WORKERS.

IN OTHER WORDS, POLICIES INTENDED TO CREATE **JOB SECURITY**...

...CAN CREATE **RIGIDITY** IN THE LABOR MARKET THAT INCREASES UNEMPLOYMENT.

MOST ECONOMISTS THINK THAT **LEAVING MARKETS ALONE** WOULD CREATE MORE JOBS.

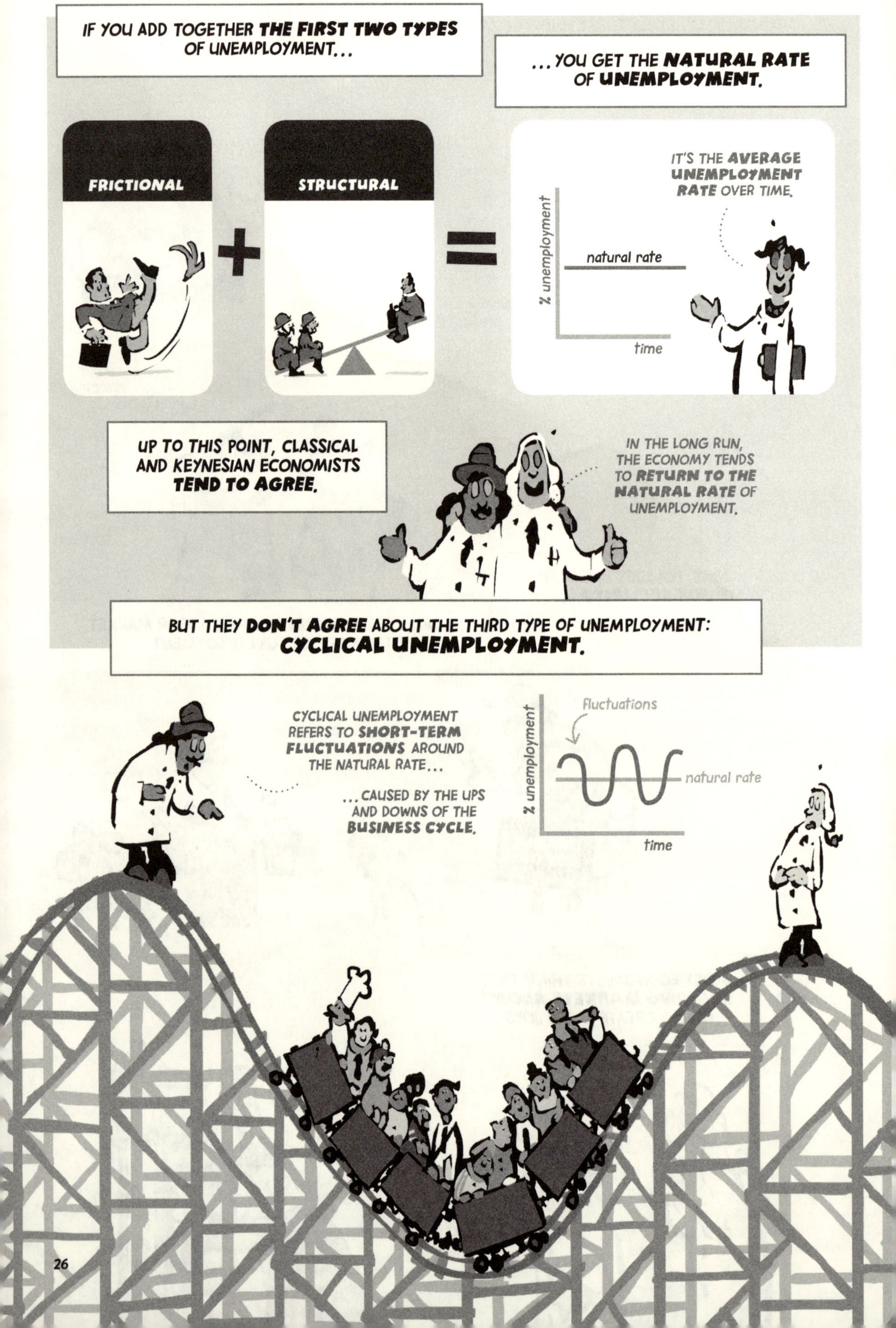

IF YOU ADD TOGETHER **THE FIRST TWO TYPES** OF UNEMPLOYMENT...

...YOU GET THE **NATURAL RATE** OF **UNEMPLOYMENT.**

IT'S THE **AVERAGE UNEMPLOYMENT RATE** OVER TIME.

UP TO THIS POINT, CLASSICAL AND KEYNESIAN ECONOMISTS **TEND TO AGREE.**

IN THE LONG RUN, THE ECONOMY TENDS TO **RETURN TO THE NATURAL RATE** OF UNEMPLOYMENT.

BUT THEY **DON'T AGREE** ABOUT THE THIRD TYPE OF UNEMPLOYMENT: **CYCLICAL UNEMPLOYMENT.**

CYCLICAL UNEMPLOYMENT REFERS TO **SHORT-TERM FLUCTUATIONS** AROUND THE NATURAL RATE...

...CAUSED BY THE UPS AND DOWNS OF THE **BUSINESS CYCLE.**

fluctuations
% unemployment
natural rate
time

CYCLICAL UNEMPLOYMENT HIGHLIGHTS THE **DIFFERENCE** BETWEEN THE CLASSICAL AND THE KEYNESIAN VIEWS.

FORCED TO CHOOSE BETWEEN **BASIC ECONOMIC THEORY**...

...AND WHAT APPEARS TO BE **A BASIC FACT OF LIFE**...

...CLASSICAL AND KEYNESIAN ECONOMISTS **HEAD IN DIFFERENT DIRECTIONS.**

KEYNESIAN ECONOMISTS STRUGGLED FOR MANY YEARS TO FIND A **THEORY** TO EXPLAIN **CYCLICAL UNEMPLOYMENT**...

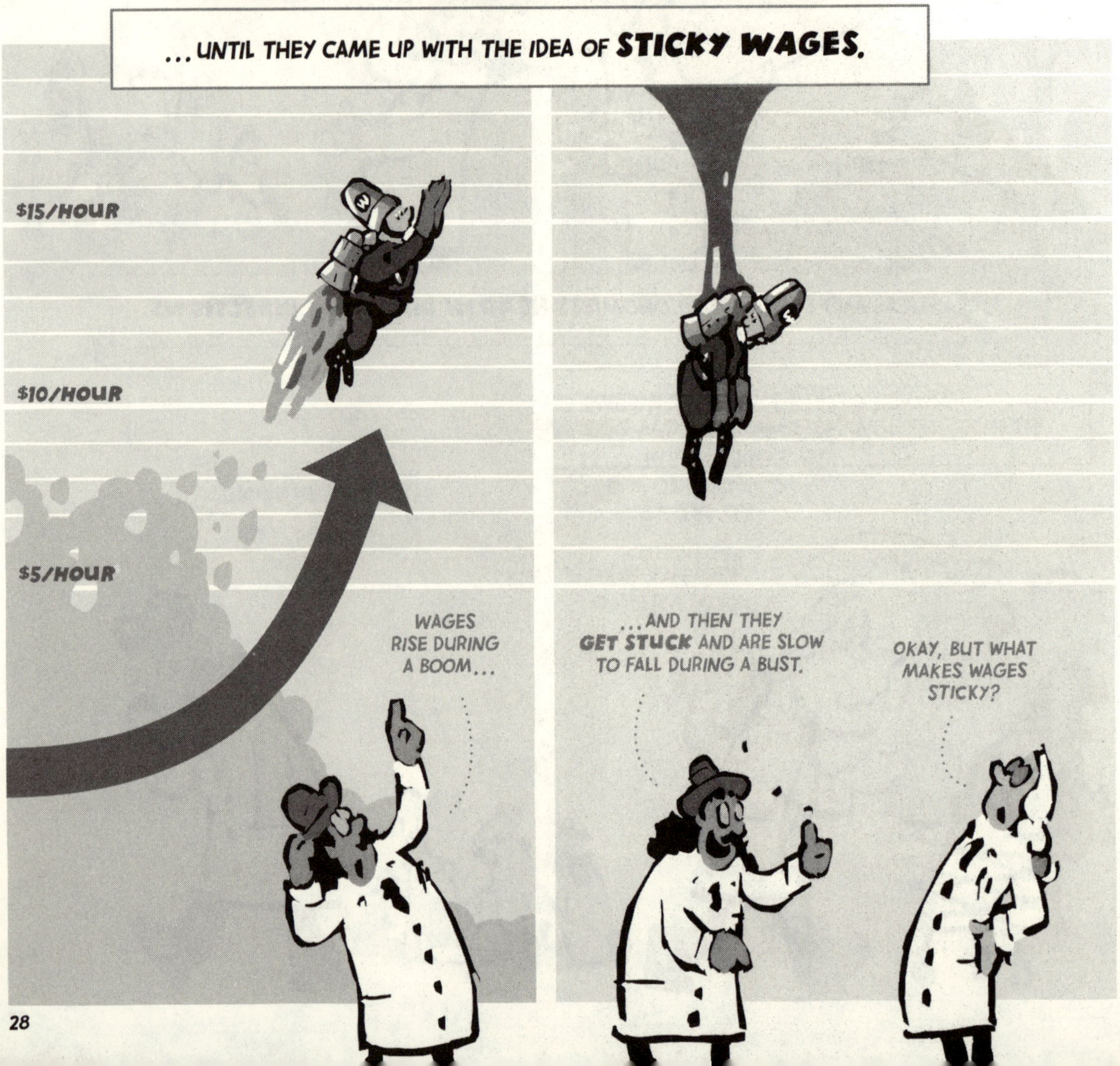

...UNTIL THEY CAME UP WITH THE IDEA OF **STICKY WAGES.**

ONE ARGUMENT FOR WHY WAGES ARE SLOW TO FALL IS THAT **JOB CONTRACTS** CAN LAST FOR **MANY YEARS.**

ANOTHER ARGUMENT IS THAT WORKERS ARE **PSYCHOLOGICALLY RESISTANT TO WAGE CUTS.**

NOT ALL MACROECONOMISTS **AGREE** THAT STICKY WAGES ARE IMPORTANT...

YOU THINK UNEMPLOYMENT GOES UP DURING RECESSIONS BECAUSE OF **STICKY WAGES?**

COME ON, **GET REAL.**

...BUT WITHOUT THEM, IT'S HARD TO COMBINE **THEORY** AND **EVIDENCE.**

UNEMPLOYMENT CONTINUES TO BE A HOT TOPIC AMONG ECONOMISTS, INCLUDING THE THREE SCHOLARS WHO WON THE 2010 NOBEL PRIZE.
FINDING A JOB CAN BE HARD.
YEAH!
AND WE CAN PROVE IT!
CONGRATULATIONS, YOU WIN THE NOBEL PRIZE!
AND, AT LEAST FOR NOW, MANY KEYNESIAN ECONOMISTS ARE QUITE ATTACHED TO THE THEORY OF STICKY WAGES.
AND WAGES AREN'T THE ONLY THINGS THAT ARE STICKY.
OTHER KINDS OF PRICES CAN BE STICKY TOO!

CHAPTER 3
MONEY

FOR MOST PEOPLE, **MONEY** IS A KEY MEASURE OF ECONOMIC SUCCESS...
...BUT FOR ECONOMISTS, **MONEY** IS MERELY SOMETHING THAT **FACILITATES TRADE.**

IT'S LIKE **OIL** THAT **LUBRICATES** THE WHOLE ECONOMY.
IT KEEPS THE GEARS **RUNNING SMOOTHLY.**

TO UNDERSTAND HOW MONEY SERVES AS A **MEDIUM OF EXCHANGE** IN AN ECONOMY, IMAGINE HOW COMPLICATED LIFE WOULD BE **WITHOUT IT.**
I'VE GOT SOME CHICKENS, BUT WHAT I REALLY WANT IS A **BIKE.**
I'VE GOT A BIKE, BUT WHAT I REALLY WANT IS SOME **SINGING LESSONS.**
I CAN TEACH YOU HOW TO SING, BUT WHAT I REALLY WANT IS A **HAIRCUT.**
NOW WE JUST NEED TO FIND **A BARBER WHO WANTS SOME CHICKENS!**

THROUGHOUT HISTORY, PEOPLE HAVE USED **ALL KINDS OF THINGS** AS MONEY.

IN MOST OF THESE CASES, THE KEY FACTOR WAS THAT "MONEY" WAS SOMETHING WITH **INTRINSIC VALUE.**

NOWADAYS, MOST MONEY IS **FIAT MONEY**, MEANING THAT IT HAS VALUE SIMPLY BECAUSE **EVERYBODY BELIEVES THAT IT DOES.**

IT MAY SEEM **CRAZY** THAT GOVERNMENTS HAVE THE POWER TO **CREATE MONEY OUT OF THIN AIR**...

...BUT IT'S **LESS CRAZY** WHEN YOU RECOGNIZE THAT THIS POWER IS OF **LIMITED VALUE.**

IN FACT, WHEN IT COMES TO LONG-RUN GROWTH, MOST ECONOMISTS SAY THAT **MONEY IS NEUTRAL**...

...OR, TO MISUSE A RELATED TERM THAT'S MORE FUN, **SUPER-NEUTRAL.**

THE THEORY OF MONEY NEUTRALITY SAYS THAT IF THE AMOUNT OF MONEY IN CIRCULATION WAS TO **DOUBLE**...

...EVERYONE WOULD MAKE **TWICE** AS MUCH MONEY...

...BUT EVERYTHING WOULD COST **TWICE** AS MUCH.

FROM THIS PERSPECTIVE, CHANGES IN THE VALUE OF A DOLLAR ARE AS **IRRELEVANT** AS CHANGING THE DEFINITION OF A FOOT TO BE **6 INCHES** INSTEAD OF 12.

IN SHORT, THE THEORY OF MONEY NEUTRALITY SAYS THAT **MONEY DOESN'T MATTER.**

THIS IDEA GOES BACK TO THE CLASSICAL ECONOMIST **ADAM SMITH** AND HIS COLLEAGUE **DAVID HUME.**

MONEY IS A **VEIL** THAT DOESN'T AFFECT THE UNDERLYING **ECONOMIC REALITY.**

YOU'RE RIGHT! MONEY IS OF **NO CONSEQUENCE!**

IN THAT CASE, CAN I HAVE YOURS?

ALMOST ALL ECONOMISTS AGREE THAT MONEY DOESN'T MATTER **IN THE LONG RUN**...
HELP!
HELP!
I TOLD YOU... ...I CAN'T HELP!
HELP!
HELP!
...BUT **IN THE SHORT RUN**, MOST ECONOMISTS—ESPECIALLY **KEYNESIANS**—BELIEVE THAT **MONEY ACTUALLY DOES MATTER!**

IN THE **LONG RUN** I'M **SUPER-NEUTRAL**...
Telephone
...BUT IN THE **SHORT RUN** I'M **MONETARY POLICY MAN**.
THEY ARGUE THAT CHANGING THE VALUE OF A DOLLAR CAN TEMPORARILY ALTER THE **UNEMPLOYMENT RATE** AND OTHER IMPORTANT ECONOMIC VARIABLES.

IN ECONOMICS JARGON, WE SAY THAT CHANGES IN **NOMINAL VARIABLES**...
...CAN AFFECT **REAL VARIABLES**.
IN PLAIN ENGLISH, THIS MEANS THAT CHANGING THE NUMBER OF INCHES IN A FOOT...
...**CAN** HELP ME DUNK!
NO WONDER **MONETARY POLICY** IS SO IMPORTANT!

MANAGING **MONETARY POLICY** IS ONE OF THE MAIN RESPONSIBILITIES OF GOVERNMENT ENTITIES CALLED **CENTRAL BANKS.**

CENTRAL BANKS CAN'T DO MUCH ABOUT ECONOMIC GROWTH IN THE **LONG RUN...**

...BUT THEY WORK HARD TO **PROMOTE MACROECONOMIC STABILITY IN THE SHORT RUN.**

TO SEE HOW CENTRAL BANKS WORK, IMAGINE A **SICK ECONOMY** THAT IS **STUCK IN THE DOLDRUMS.**

INVESTMENT IS DOWN.

EMPLOYMENT IS DOWN.

THIS IS THE **WORST PARTY EVER!**

THE CENTRAL BANK CAN STIMULATE THIS ECONOMY BY **INCREASING THE MONEY SUPPLY.**

THIS GIVES BUSINESSES AND CONSUMERS INCENTIVES TO **INCREASE SPENDING IN THE SHORT RUN...**

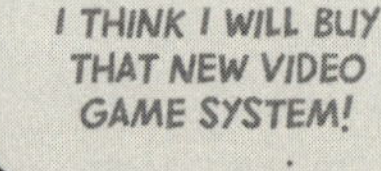

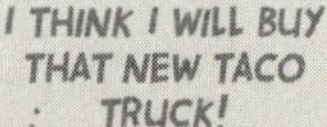

...AND THAT EXTRA SPENDING HELPS **KICK-START ECONOMIC GROWTH.**

WE'LL GO INTO THE DETAILS ON THE NEXT FEW PAGES.

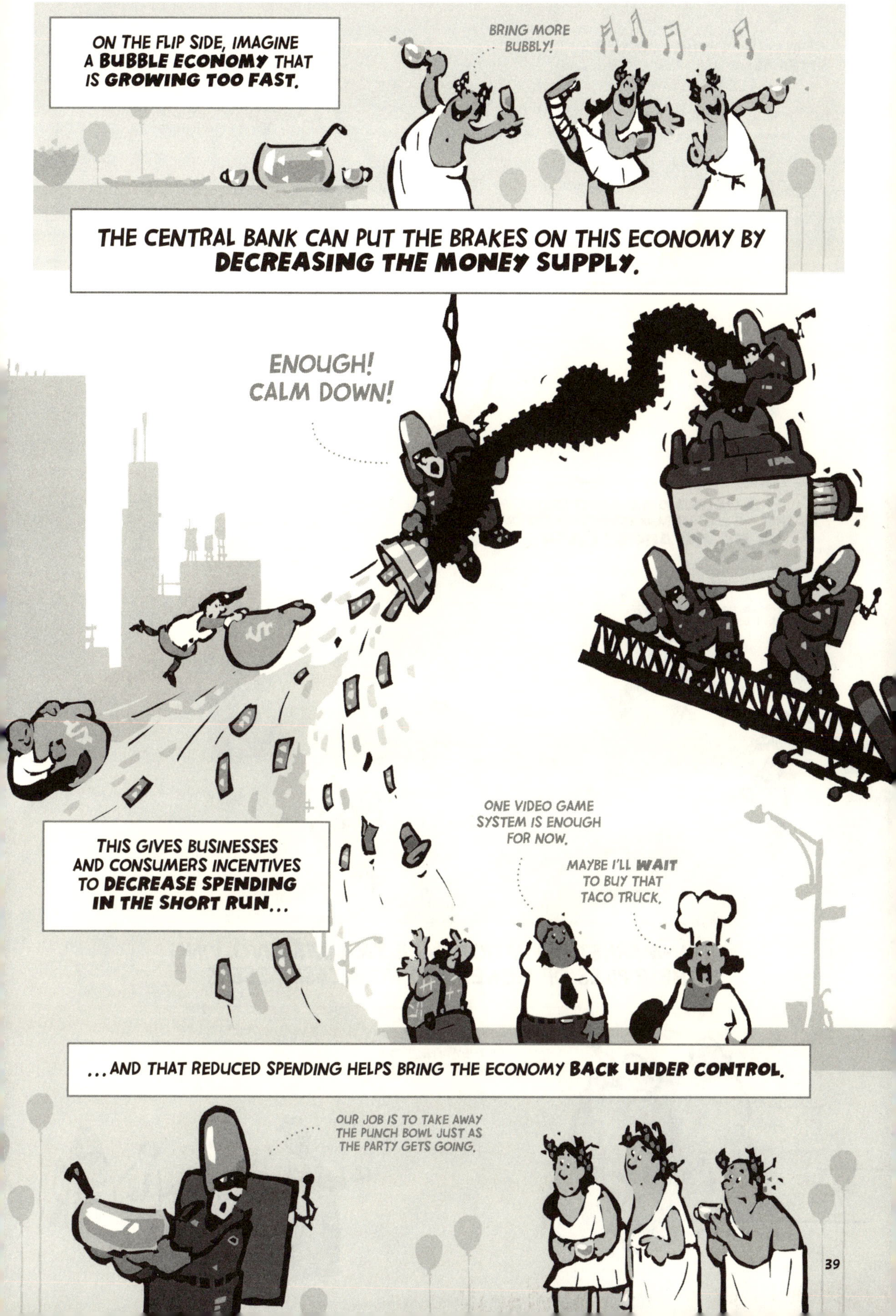

ON THE FLIP SIDE, IMAGINE A **BUBBLE ECONOMY** THAT IS **GROWING TOO FAST.**

THE CENTRAL BANK CAN PUT THE BRAKES ON THIS ECONOMY BY **DECREASING THE MONEY SUPPLY.**

ENOUGH! CALM DOWN!

THIS GIVES BUSINESSES AND CONSUMERS INCENTIVES TO **DECREASE SPENDING IN THE SHORT RUN...**

...AND THAT REDUCED SPENDING HELPS BRING THE ECONOMY **BACK UNDER CONTROL.**

OF COURSE, CENTRAL BANKS DON'T **LITERALLY** USE HELICOPTERS AND SUCTION PUMPS.

INSTEAD, THEY CHANGE THE MONEY SUPPLY USING **OPEN-MARKET OPERATIONS.**

TO UNDERSTAND THESE, NOTE FIRST THAT THE CENTRAL BANK ESSENTIALLY SITS ON **A MOUNTAIN OF CASH**...

...AND ALSO ON A MOUNTAIN OF **NON-CASH ASSETS** LIKE GOLD AND **GOVERNMENT BONDS.**

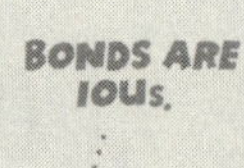

OPEN-MARKET OPERATIONS ARE **TRADES** INVOLVING THESE PILES OF MONEY AND NON-CASH ASSETS.

OPEN-MARKET OPERATIONS WORK BECAUSE OF **SUPPLY AND DEMAND**, IN THIS CASE THE SUPPLY OF AND DEMAND FOR MONEY.

THE **DEMAND FOR MONEY** IS DETERMINED BY THE **INTEREST RATE**, WHICH YOU CAN THINK OF AS THE "PRICE" OF MONEY...

AT **HIGHER** INTEREST RATES, PEOPLE WANT TO **CARRY AROUND LESS MONEY**.

AT **LOWER** INTEREST RATES, PEOPLE ARE WILLING TO **HOLD ON TO MORE MONEY**.

Interest Rate

DEMAND CURVE

YOU SHOULD PUT YOUR EXTRA MONEY INTO AN INTEREST-BEARING SAVINGS ACCOUNT.

...AND THE **SUPPLY OF MONEY** IS DETERMINED BY THE CENTRAL BANK.

WHEN THE CENTRAL BANK WANTS TO **STIMULATE** THE ECONOMY...

...IT USES ITS PILE OF CASH TO **BUY BONDS.**

THE RESULT OF THESE OPEN-MARKET OPERATIONS IS **MORE MONEY IN CIRCULATION.**

THE MONEY SUPPLY **INCREASES.**

Interest Rate

OLD SUPPLY

NEW SUPPLY

Quantity of Money

AN INCREASE IN THE MONEY SUPPLY **LOWERS INTEREST RATES...**

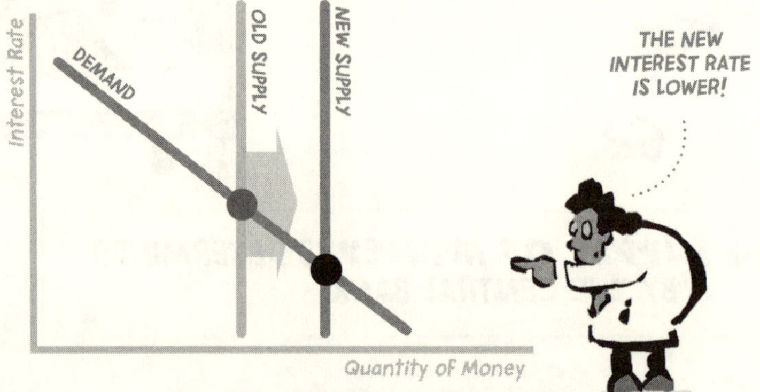

...AND THAT **STIMULATES** THE ECONOMY BY ENCOURAGING **MORE BORROWING** AND **MORE SPENDING.**

WHEN THE CENTRAL BANK WANTS TO **CALM DOWN** THE ECONOMY...

...IT **SELLS BONDS** FROM ITS PILE OF NON-CASH ASSETS.

THE RESULT OF THESE OPEN-MARKET OPERATIONS IS **LESS MONEY IN CIRCULATION**.

A DECREASE IN THE MONEY SUPPLY **RAISES INTEREST RATES**...

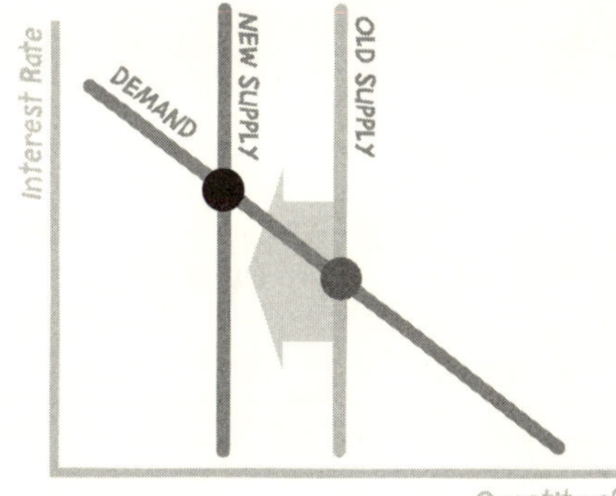

...AND THAT **COOLS DOWN** THE ECONOMY BY ENCOURAGING **LESS BORROWING** AND **LESS SPENDING**.

BUT REMEMBER, THESE ARE **SHORT-RUN** EFFECTS.

IN THE LONG RUN, YOU CAN'T GET RICH BY PRINTING MONEY...

CHAPTER 4
INFLATION

INFLATION IS A GENERAL **INCREASE IN PRICES** OVER TIME OR, EQUIVALENTLY, A GENERAL **DECREASE** IN THE **VALUE OF MONEY.**

THE MOST COMMON WAY TO **MEASURE INFLATION** IS WITH THE **CONSUMER PRICE INDEX (CPI).**

THE CPI TAKES A **REPRESENTATIVE BUNDLE** OF GOODS AND SERVICES...

...AND TRACKS HOW THE **PRICE** OF THAT BUNDLE **CHANGES OVER TIME.**

FOR EXAMPLE, IF THE BUNDLE COST **$100 IN 1920...**

...AND **$1,000 IN 2010...**

GIVE ME A BAR OF SOAP, A CAMPING TENT, A CANDY BAR, AND THREE MONTHS' RENT...

THAT'LL BE **$1,000.**

CPI 2010

...THEN WE WOULD SAY THAT THE **PRICE LEVEL IN 2010** WAS **10 TIMES** WHAT IT WAS **IN 1920.**

ECONOMISTS WHO **CALCULATE INFLATION** ENCOUNTER PLENTY OF DIFFICULTIES...

...BUT THE **BASIC IDEA** IS STRAIGHTFORWARD:

THE FACT THAT THE CPI **DOUBLED** BETWEEN 1985 AND 2009...

...MEANS THAT, **ON AVERAGE**, PRICES IN 2009 WERE DOUBLE WHAT THEY WERE IN 1985.

A **DOUBLING** OF PRICES IN **24 YEARS** SOUNDS LIKE A LOT OF INFLATION...

...BUT IN FACT IT AVERAGES OUT TO ONLY ABOUT **3% PER YEAR.**

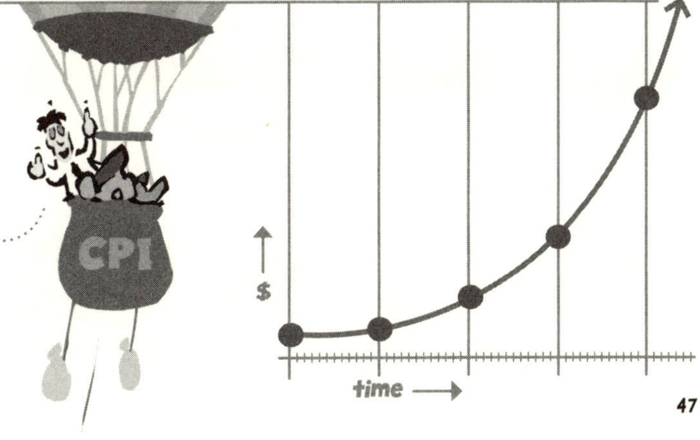

THE **EASY QUESTION** ABOUT INFLATION IS **WHY IT HAPPENS.**

TO QUOTE **MILTON FRIEDMAN**, INFLATION IS "ALWAYS AND EVERYWHERE A **MONETARY PHENOMENON.**"

THE **HARD QUESTION** ABOUT INFLATION IS **WHY IT MATTERS.**

THIS IS A HARD QUESTION BECAUSE ECONOMISTS THINK THAT **MONEY IS NEUTRAL** IN THE LONG RUN.

IN FACT, MANY ECONOMISTS THINK THAT THE GENERAL PUBLIC SUFFERS FROM **MONEY ILLUSION.**

MONEY ILLUSION HAPPENS WHEN PEOPLE THINK IN **NOMINAL TERMS...**

...RATHER THAN IN **REAL TERMS.**

MONEY ILLUSION SHOWS WHY INFLATION MATTERS IN THE REAL WORLD: IT CAN CAUSE **CONFUSION AND INSTABILITY.**

TO AVOID SUFFERING FROM MONEY ILLUSION, ECONOMISTS STUDY HOW PRICES CHANGE **IN REAL TERMS.**

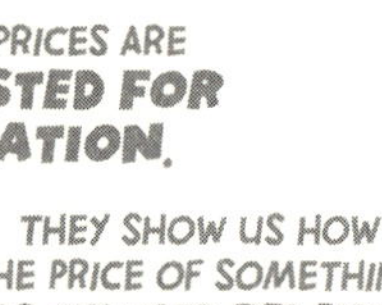

REAL PRICES ARE **ADJUSTED FOR INFLATION.**

THEY SHOW US HOW THE PRICE OF SOMETHING HAS CHANGED **RELATIVE TO THE OVERALL PRICE LEVEL.**

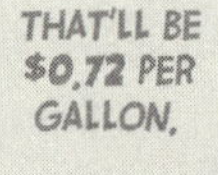

FOR EXAMPLE, COMPARE THE PRICE OF MILK IN **1920**...

...WITH THE PRICE OF MILK IN **2010.**

BASED ON THIS COMPARISON OF **NOMINAL PRICES,** IT LOOKS AS IF MILK HAS GOTTEN A LOT MORE EXPENSIVE.

BUT IF WE **ADJUST FOR INFLATION** BETWEEN 1920 AND 2010...

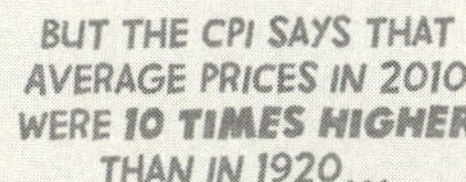

...WE SEE THAT **THE REAL PRICE OF MILK** HAS ACTUALLY **FALLEN.**

WHAT THIS MEANS IS THAT THE PRICES OF MOST OTHER THINGS HAVE **GONE UP MORE THAN THE PRICE OF MILK.**

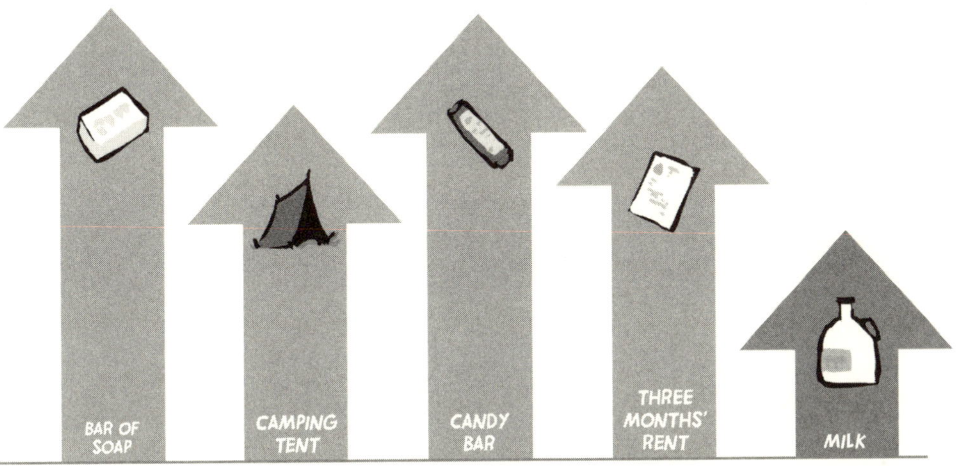

YOU CAN ALSO GRASP THE **INTUITION** HERE BY THINKING ABOUT PRICES IN TERMS OF **WORK HOURS.**

ECONOMISTS ALSO ADJUST **INTEREST RATES** TO ACCOUNT FOR INFLATION.

OTHERWISE WE CAN'T ACCURATELY COMPARE **MONEY TODAY**...

...WITH **MONEY TOMORROW**.

THE **NOMINAL INTEREST RATE** TELLS YOU THE GROWTH RATE OF MONEY IN THE BANK...

...BUT YOUR **PURCHASING POWER**—YOUR ABILITY TO **BUY STUFF**—GROWS MORE SLOWLY BECAUSE OF INFLATION.

WOW, **MY MONEY** IS **GROWING FAST!**

PRICES ARE GOING UP, TOO, SO YOUR MONEY ISN'T WORTH AS MUCH...

...AND THAT'S WHY WE NEED TO **ADJUST FOR INFLATION**.

THE REAL INTEREST RATE TELLS YOU HOW MUCH YOUR **PURCHASING POWER** IS GROWING.

THERE'S A HANDY **RULE OF THUMB** THAT RELATES **NOMINAL** AND **REAL** INTEREST RATES.

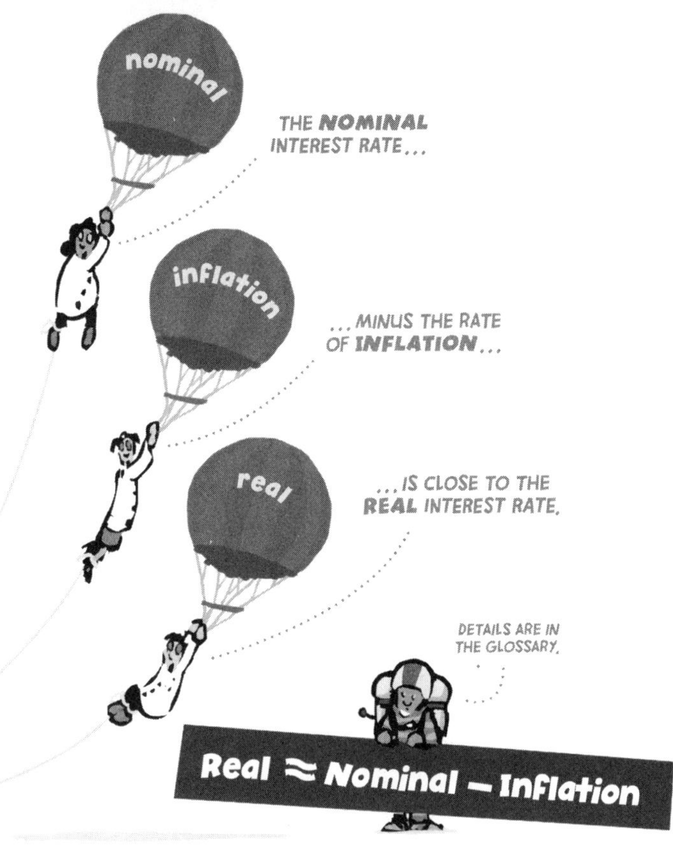

FOR EXAMPLE, IF THE NOMINAL INTEREST RATE IS **5%**...

...AND INFLATION IS **3%**...

...THE REAL INTEREST RATE IS ABOUT **2%**.

AS WITH PRICES, INTEREST RATES ARE USUALLY GIVEN IN **NOMINAL** TERMS...

...BUT IT'S THE **REAL** INTEREST RATE THAT **DRIVES ECONOMIC DECISIONS.**

WE'VE SEEN THAT **SMALL AMOUNTS** OF INFLATION CAN CAUSE CONFUSION AND INSTABILITY...

...BUT **LARGE AMOUNTS** CAN CAUSE SERIOUS DAMAGE TO ENTIRE ECONOMIES.

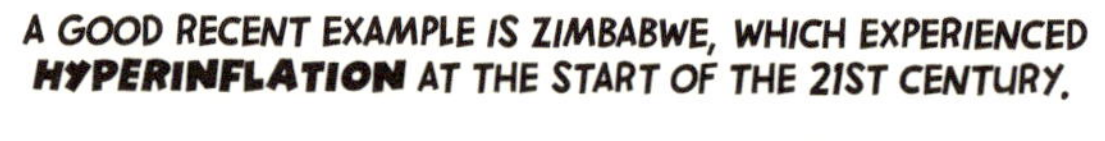

A GOOD RECENT EXAMPLE IS ZIMBABWE, WHICH EXPERIENCED **HYPERINFLATION** AT THE START OF THE 21ST CENTURY.

EVEN MORE MODERATE INFLATION—LIKE **13%** IN THE U.S. IN 1979—IS RISKY BECAUSE IT CAN GENERATE A **WAGE-PRICE SPIRAL.**

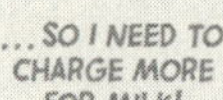

ECONOMISTS GENERALLY AGREE THAT INFLATION ANYWHERE NEAR **DOUBLE DIGITS** IS TROUBLE.

BUT INFLATION IS NOT THE ONLY TROUBLE WITH **CHANGES IN THE PRICE LEVEL.**

THERE'S ALSO **DEFLATION**, A GENERAL **DECREASE** IN PRICES OVER TIME.

DEFLATIONARY PERIODS LIKE THE **GREAT DEPRESSION** AND THE **"LOST DECADES"** IN JAPAN AT THE TURN OF THE 21ST CENTURY...

...ARE PERHAPS EVEN **MORE DANGEROUS** THAN INFLATIONARY PERIODS.

BECAUSE HIGH INFLATION AND DEFLATION ARE **BOTH BAD**, MONETARY POLICY MAKERS HAVE TO BE **VERY CAREFUL**.

MOST ECONOMISTS THINK THAT THE BEST TARGET IS **2–3% INFLATION PER YEAR**.

AIMING FOR INFLATION OF 2–3% PER YEAR CAN ALSO PROVIDE BENEFITS IN DEALING WITH **UNEMPLOYMENT** CAUSED BY **STICKY WAGES.**

DURING A RECESSION, WAGES CAN **GET STUCK** AT LEVELS THAT ARE **TOO HIGH**...

...AND A SMALL AMOUNT OF INFLATION CAN HELP **BALANCE** SUPPLY AND DEMAND.

FOR EXAMPLE, WORKERS WHO ARE **PSYCHOLOGICALLY OPPOSED TO WAGE CUTS**...

...DON'T SEEM TO MIND IT WHEN THEIR WAGES INCREASE BY 1% BUT INFLATION IS 3%.

OVERALL, ECONOMISTS VIEW **INFLATION** THE WAY DOCTORS VIEW **ALCOHOL:**

A LITTLE BIT MAY ACTUALLY BE **A GOOD THING...**

...BUT A LOT IS BAD BAD BAD.

CHAPTER 5
GROSS DOMESTIC PRODUCT (GDP)

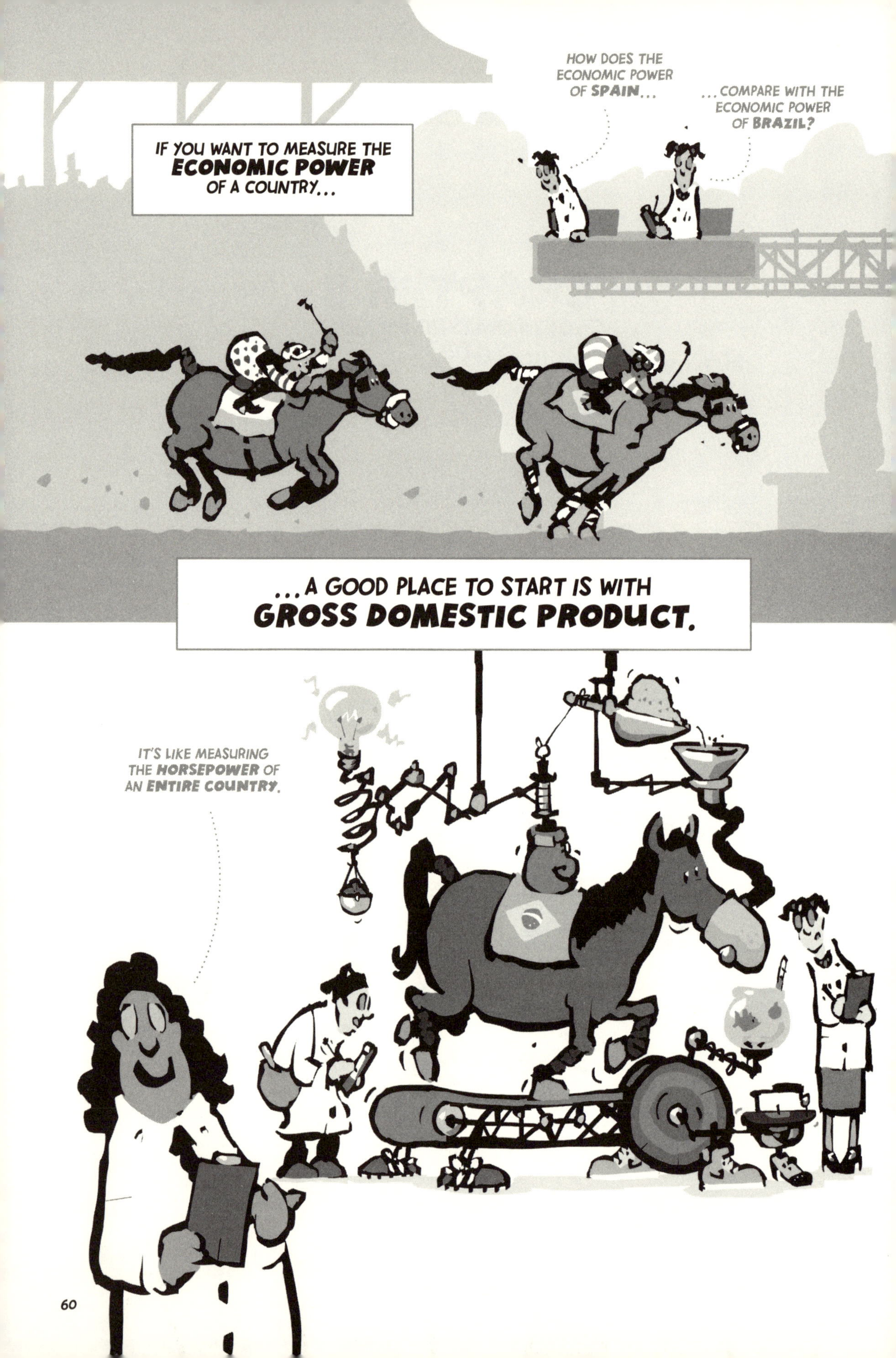

...A GOOD PLACE TO START IS WITH **GROSS DOMESTIC PRODUCT.**

IT'S LIKE MEASURING THE **HORSEPOWER** OF AN **ENTIRE COUNTRY.**

IN THIS CHAPTER WE'LL SEE HOW GDP SHEDS LIGHT ON **SHORT-RUN STABILITY...**

...AND ON **LONG-RUN GROWTH.**

BUT FIRST, LET'S LEARN HOW TO **CALCULATE GDP.**

1 THE VALUE-ADDED APPROACH

JUST AS WE CAN MEASURE THE **VALUE ADDED** TO THE MARKET ECONOMY EACH YEAR BY A **COMPANY'S** LABOR AND CAPITAL...

LAST YEAR WE SPENT **$200,000** ON FLOUR, CHEESE, TOMATOES, AND ELECTRICITY...

...AND WE PRODUCED PIZZA WORTH **$500,000**...

...SO OUR COMPANY'S **VALUE ADDED** WAS **$300,000!**

...**GDP** MEASURES THE **VALUE ADDED** TO THE MARKET ECONOMY BY AN **ENTIRE COUNTRY'S** LABOR AND CAPITAL.

LAST YEAR WE SPENT **$200 BILLION** ON **IMPORTS**...

...AND WE PRODUCED **FINAL GOODS AND SERVICES** WORTH **$500 BILLION**...

...SO OUR COUNTRY'S **VALUE ADDED** WAS **$300 BILLION.**

THE VALUE-ADDED APPROACH IS THE **MOST INTUITIVE** WAY TO THINK ABOUT GDP.

GDP = Final Outputs − Imports

2 THE NATIONAL INCOME APPROACH

EVERY DOLLAR OF VALUE ADDED **ENDS UP IN SOMEBODY'S POCKET**, SO GDP ALSO MEASURES **NATIONAL INCOME.**

OUR **TOTAL VALUE ADDED** OF $300 BILLION...

...INCLUDES **LABOR INCOME** OF $200 BILLION...

...AND **CAPITAL INCOME** OF $100 BILLION.

THE NATIONAL INCOME APPROACH IS TO **FOLLOW THE MONEY.**

GDP = Labor Income + Capital Income

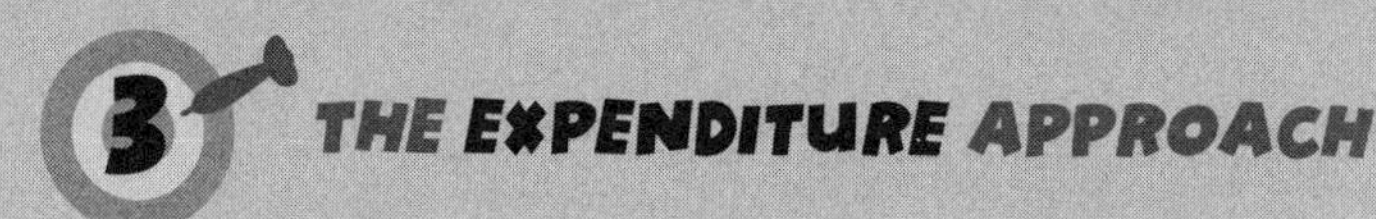

THE EXPENDITURE APPROACH

TO SEE HOW **GDP** RELATES TO **EXPENDITURES**, WE START WITH THE VALUE-ADDED APPROACH...

GDP = Final Outputs − Imports

...AND THEN NOTE THAT EVERY DOLLAR SPENT ON FINAL OUTPUTS **COMES FROM SOMEBODY'S POCKET**.

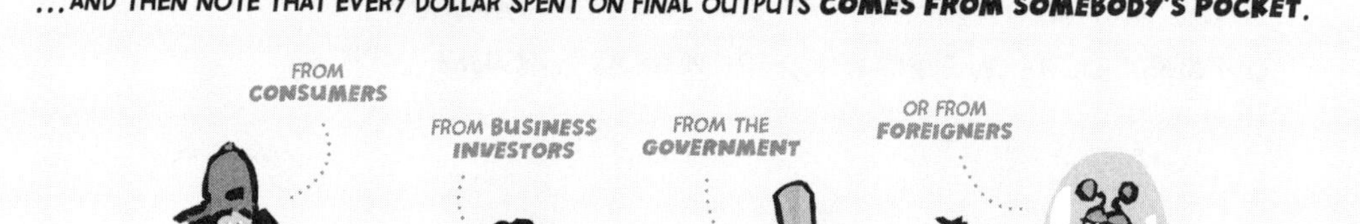

$$\text{GDP} = \overbrace{C + I + G + \text{Exports}}^{\text{Final Outputs}} - \text{Imports}$$

APPLYING THESE FORMULAS ISN'T EASY, WHICH IS WHY **RICHARD STONE** AND **SIMON KUZNETS** WON NOBEL PRIZES FOR WORKING OUT ALL THE COMPLICATIONS.

HOWEVER YOU MEASURE IT, **GDP** GIVES MACROECONOMISTS A WAY TO **TELL A STORY** ABOUT AN **ENTIRE ECONOMY.**

GDP SHEDS LIGHT ON EVERYTHING FROM **HEALTH CARE...**

...TO THE **SIZE OF GOVERNMENT...**

...TO THE **NATIONAL DEBT.**

NO WONDER GDP IS THE **MOST IMPORTANT STATISTIC** IN MACROECONOMICS!

THERE ARE ALSO **TWO VARIATIONS** ON GDP THAT HELP US TELL THE STORY OF AN ECONOMY.

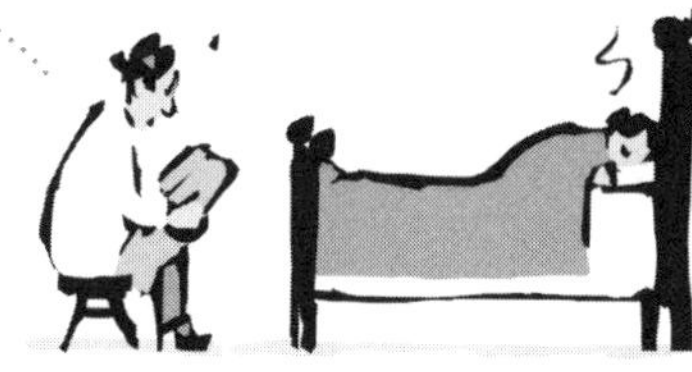

REAL GDP
ADJUSTS FOR INFLATION.

REAL GDP PER CAPITA
ADJUSTS FOR INFLATION AND POPULATION.

THE BEST WAY TO TELL HOW **STABLE** AN ECONOMY IS IN THE **SHORT TERM**...

...IS TO LOOK AT **REAL GDP**.

ECONOMISTS COULD ADJUST GDP FOR INFLATION USING THE **CONSUMER PRICE INDEX**...

...BUT IN PRACTICE THEY USE A RELATED MEASURE CALLED THE **GDP DEFLATOR**.

ONCE WE ADJUST FOR INFLATION, **RECESSIONS** SHOW UP AS **DECLINES IN REAL GDP...**

...AND **DEPRESSIONS** SHOW UP AS **STEEP AND PROLONGED DECLINES IN REAL GDP.**

SINCE THE GREAT DEPRESSION, THE U.S. ECONOMY HAS GONE THROUGH THE UPS AND DOWNS OF THE **BUSINESS CYCLE** ABOUT A DOZEN TIMES.

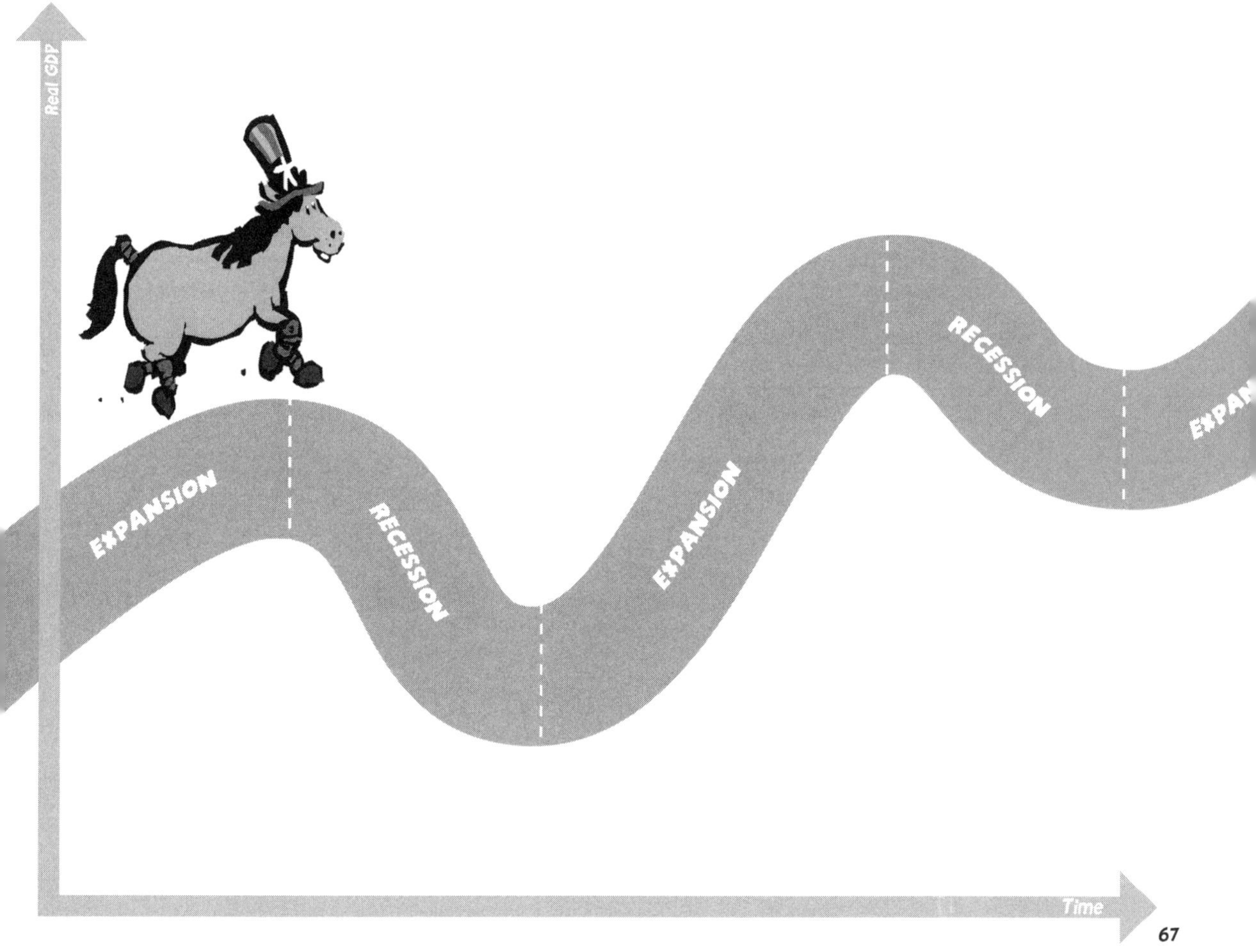

Real GDP

EXPANSION

RECESSION

EXPANSION

RECESSION

Time

THE BEST WAY TO TELL IF AN ECONOMY IS **GROWING** IN THE **LONG RUN**...

...IS TO LOOK AT **REAL GDP PER CAPITA.**

FOR EXAMPLE, HERE'S A BRIEF ECONOMIC HISTORY OF **POSTWAR JAPAN.**

AFTER WORLD WAR II, THE JAPANESE ECONOMY WAS IN SHAMBLES.

IT'S HARD TO CREATE VALUE ADDED WHEN EVERYTHING IS IN RUINS.

THEN REAL GDP PER CAPITA GREW BY AN AMAZING **6% PER YEAR** FROM 1950 TO 1991...

...AND THEN GREW BY **LESS THAN 1% PER YEAR** DURING THE "LOST DECADES" OF THE 1990s AND 2000s.

EVEN MORE FASCINATING IS THE STORY OF **CHINA**, WHICH HAD THE WORLD'S HIGHEST REAL GDP PER CAPITA IN THE **14TH CENTURY**.

OVER THE NEXT 600 YEARS, HOWEVER, REAL GDP PER CAPITA **SOARED IN EUROPE**...

...AND **STAGNATED IN CHINA**.

THEN CAME THE **ECONOMIC REFORMS** OF 1978...

...AND REAL GDP PER CAPITA IN CHINA HAS BEEN ON THE **COMEBACK TRAIL** EVER SINCE.

ONE CONCERN IS THAT GDP FOCUSES ON THE **MARKET ECONOMY**, WHICH MEANS IT IGNORES **NON-MARKET ISSUES**...

...LIKE UNPAID **HOUSEHOLD LABOR**...

...AND **ENVIRONMENTAL QUALITY**.

ANOTHER MAJOR CONCERN IS THAT GDP DOESN'T TELL US ANYTHING ABOUT THE **DISTRIBUTION** OF ECONOMIC POWER.

CHINA'S ECONOMIC GROWTH HAS CREATED A HUGE GAP BETWEEN **RICH AND POOR**...

IN 2005, ABOUT 36% OF THE POPULATION WAS LIVING ON LESS THAN $2 A DAY.

...AND IN THE U.S. THE "GREAT RECESSION" OF 2007–2009 ENDED IN A **JOBLESS RECOVERY**.

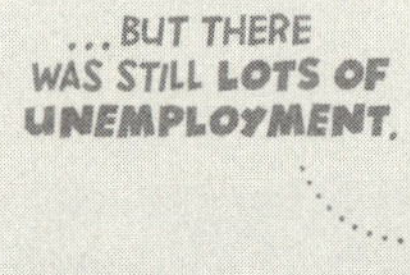

MACROECONOMISTS ARE OF COURSE AWARE OF GDP'S **LIMITATIONS**.

IN POOR COUNTRIES THE **HUMAN DEVELOPMENT INDEX** MAY BE A BETTER ALTERNATIVE...

...AND IN RICH COUNTRIES SOME ECONOMISTS ARE QUESTIONING THE CONNECTION BETWEEN **GDP** AND **QUALITY OF LIFE**.

IN BOTH CASES, THE UNDERLYING ISSUE IS THAT **ECONOMIC POWER** IS AN INCOMPLETE MEASURE OF THE **HUMAN CONDITION**.

IN SUMMARY, **GDP ISN'T PERFECT**...

...BUT IT DOES GIVE US A **NUMERICAL SNAPSHOT** OF A COUNTRY'S ECONOMY...

...AND SOMETIMES **A NUMBER** IS WORTH A **THOUSAND CARTOONS.**

All values are in terms of purchasing power parity, which you can read about in the glossary.

CHAPTER 6
THE ROLE OF GOVERNMENT

IF THE MACROECONOMY IS **LIKE A FAMILY**...

...THEN YOU CAN THINK OF THE **GOVERNMENT** AS A **PARENT**...
WHO'S IN CHARGE HERE?

UM, I GUESS I AM.

...FOR **BETTER**...
AFTER HOMEWORK REVIEW, LET'S GO FOR **ICE CREAM!**

...OR FOR **WORSE**.
I WANT SOME ICE CREAM.
TOO BAD, WE'RE GOING FOR **CIGARETTES** AND **BOOZE**.

OF COURSE, PARENTS AREN'T **ENTIRELY RESPONSIBLE** FOR THEIR CHILDREN.

SIMILARLY, GOVERNMENTS AREN'T **ENTIRELY RESPONSIBLE** FOR THE ECONOMY...

...BUT THEY DO HAVE A LOT OF INFLUENCE ON **SHORT-RUN STABILITY** AND **LONG-RUN GROWTH**.

WE'VE ALREADY SEEN ONE IMPORTANT ROLE FOR THE GOVERNMENT IN PROMOTING SHORT-TERM STABILITY: **MONETARY POLICY.**

DURING A DOWNTURN THE GOVERNMENT'S CENTRAL BANK CAN STIMULATE THE ECONOMY BY **INCREASING THE MONEY SUPPLY...**

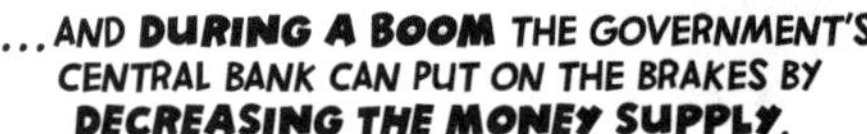

...AND **DURING A BOOM** THE GOVERNMENT'S CENTRAL BANK CAN PUT ON THE BRAKES BY **DECREASING THE MONEY SUPPLY.**

ECONOMISTS AGREE THAT MONETARY POLICY IS THE **FIRST LINE OF DEFENSE** AGAINST SHORT-TERM INSTABILITY.

BUT IF MONETARY POLICY ISN'T ENOUGH, THERE'S A BACKUP PLAN: **FISCAL POLICY.**

LIKE MONETARY POLICY, **FISCAL POLICY** IS A WAY FOR THE GOVERNMENT TO **PROMOTE SHORT-RUN STABILITY.**

UNLIKE MONETARY POLICY, FISCAL POLICY USES **CHANGES IN TAXES AND SPENDING** IN ORDER TO INFLUENCE THE ECONOMY.

GOVERNMENTS OFTEN TRY TO **BOOST THE ECONOMY** DURING DOWNTURNS BY **INCREASING SPENDING** OR **CUTTING TAXES...**

...AND PROGRAMS LIKE **UNEMPLOYMENT BENEFITS** HELP TO **AUTOMATICALLY STABILIZE** THE ECONOMY THROUGHOUT THE BUSINESS CYCLE.

IF YOU THINK OF THE GOVERNMENT AS A PARENT, **FISCAL POLICY** IS PRETTY STRAIGHTFORWARD.

DURING A RECESSION THE GOVERNMENT CAN USE FISCAL POLICY TO TRY TO **BOOST** ECONOMIC ACTIVITY...

...JUST AS A **PARENT** TRIES TO **GIVE EXTRA FOOD TO AN UNDERWEIGHT CHILD.**

AND DURING A BOOM THE GOVERNMENT CAN USE FISCAL POLICY TO TRY TO **SLOW** ECONOMIC ACTIVITY...

...JUST AS A PARENT TRIES TO GET AN **OVERWEIGHT CHILD** TO ADOPT A MORE **HEALTHY DIET.**

MORE SPECIFICALLY, THE IDEA OF FISCAL POLICY IS TO **CREATE BUDGET DEFICITS DURING RECESSIONS...**

...AND TO **CREATE BUDGET SURPLUSES DURING BOOM YEARS.**

IN AN IDEAL WORLD THESE ANNUAL DEFICITS AND SURPLUSES WOULD **BALANCE EACH OTHER OUT** IN THE LONG RUN...

...BUT **IN REALITY** IT **HASN'T WORKED OUT THAT WAY.**

AS A RESULT, SHORT-RUN FISCAL POLICY IS INCREASINGLY THREATENED BY THE ACCUMULATION OF **LONG-RUN GOVERNMENT DEBT.**

IF YOU BORROW TOO MUCH MONEY **WHEN YOU DON'T NEED IT...**

...YOU MIGHT NOT BE ABLE TO BORROW **WHEN YOU DO NEED IT.**

GOVERNMENTS ALSO HAVE A LOT OF INFLUENCE ON **THE SECOND BIG GOAL OF MACROECONOMICS.**

JUST AS **GOOD PARENTS** CAN HELP THEIR CHILDREN SUCCEED...

...GOVERNMENTS CAN PROMOTE **LONG-RUN GROWTH**...

...BY ESTABLISHING AND PROTECTING **PROPERTY RIGHTS**...

...BY PROMOTING **INNOVATION** AND PROTECTING **COMPETITION**...

...BY MAKING SMART PUBLIC INVESTMENTS IN **INFRASTRUCTURE** AND **EDUCATION**...

...AND BY DEALING WITH **POLLUTION.**

SOME ECONOMISTS ARGUE THAT GOVERNMENTS SHOULD DO **EVEN MORE.**

AS WE LEARNED IN MICROECONOMICS, EVEN WELL-FUNCTIONING MARKETS CAN GENERATE **TREMENDOUS INEQUALITY.**

GOOD GOVERNMENTS CAN TRY TO IMPROVE MATTERS BY TAKING STEPS TO **ALLEVIATE POVERTY.**

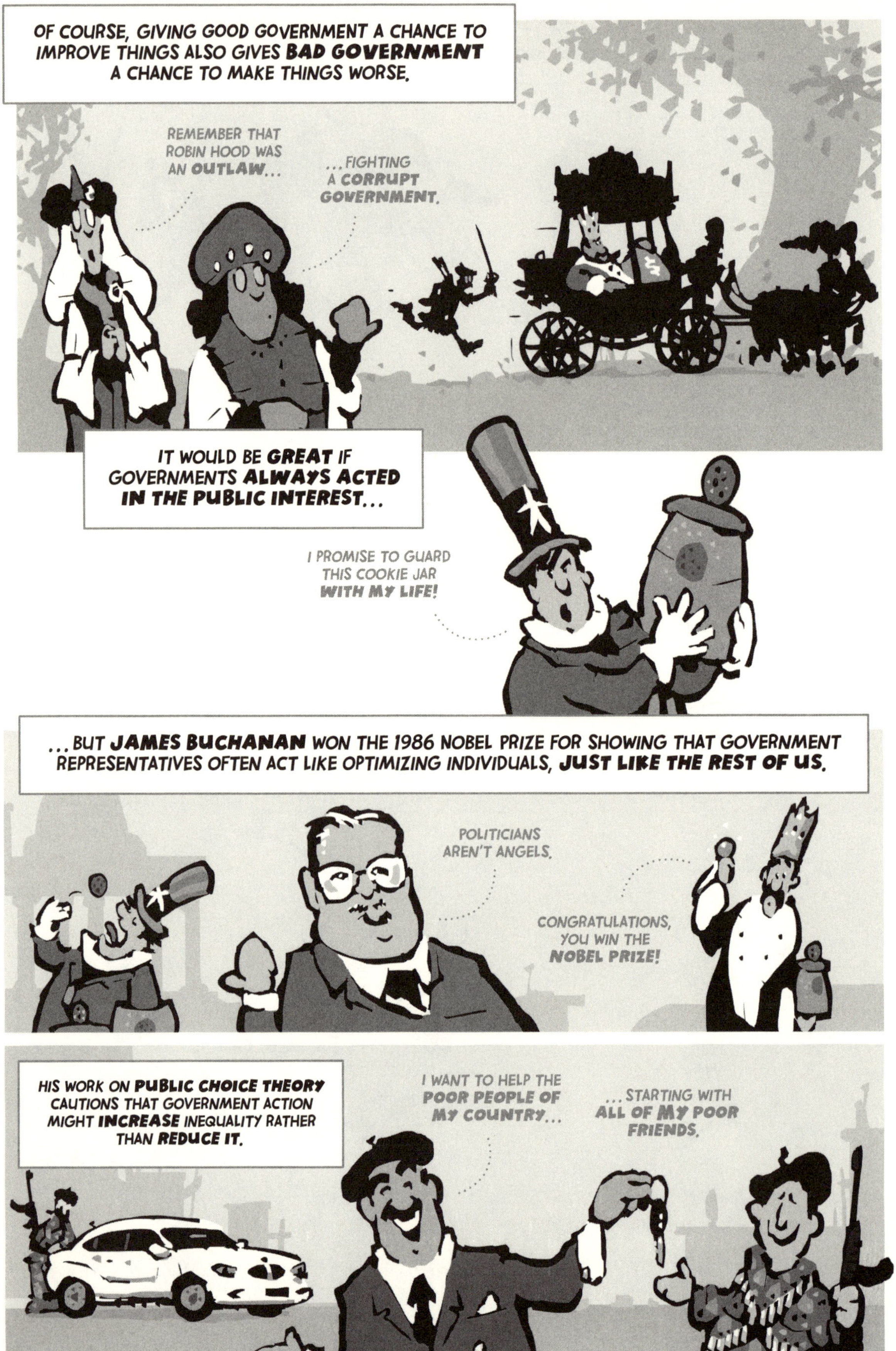

OF COURSE, GIVING GOOD GOVERNMENT A CHANCE TO IMPROVE THINGS ALSO GIVES **BAD GOVERNMENT** A CHANCE TO MAKE THINGS WORSE.

REMEMBER THAT ROBIN HOOD WAS AN **OUTLAW**...

...FIGHTING A **CORRUPT GOVERNMENT**.

IT WOULD BE **GREAT** IF GOVERNMENTS **ALWAYS ACTED IN THE PUBLIC INTEREST**...

I PROMISE TO GUARD THIS COOKIE JAR **WITH MY LIFE!**

...BUT **JAMES BUCHANAN** WON THE 1986 NOBEL PRIZE FOR SHOWING THAT GOVERNMENT REPRESENTATIVES OFTEN ACT LIKE OPTIMIZING INDIVIDUALS, **JUST LIKE THE REST OF US**.

EVEN **WELL-INTENTIONED GOVERNMENTS**, LIKE WELL-INTENTIONED PARENTS, CAN SOMETIMES MAKE LIFE PRETTY **UNBEARABLE.**

SUPPLY-SIDE ECONOMISTS EMPHASIZE THE ECONOMIC DAMAGE THAT GOVERNMENTS CAN CAUSE...

...AND CONCLUDE THAT THE **INVISIBLE HAND** DOESN'T NEED MUCH **GOVERNMENT ASSISTANCE.**

THE CHALLENGE FOR GOVERNMENTS, LIKE PARENTS, IS FINDING A GOOD MIDDLE GROUND BETWEEN BEING **TOO HANDS-OFF**...

...AND BEING **TOO HANDS-ON**.

THE EXTENT OF GOVERNMENT INVOLVEMENT IS OFTEN MEASURED BY LOOKING AT GOVERNMENT SPENDING AS A PERCENTAGE OF **GDP**...

...AND ALSO BY LOOKING AT THE EXTENT OF **GOVERNMENT REGULATIONS**.

ULTIMATELY, GOVERNMENTS NEED TO STRIKE A BALANCE...
...BETWEEN THE JUNGLE...
EVERY BEAST FOR HERSELF!
SURVIVAL OF THE FITTEST!
YOU'RE ON YOUR OWN!
SINK OR SWIM!
KILL OR BE KILLED!
NO Rules
...AND THE ZOO.
WELFARE FROM THE CRADLE TO THE GRAVE.
DON'T WORRY, WE'RE IN CHARGE.
NO SWIMMING, AND DEFINITELY NO KILLING.
Nothing but Rules

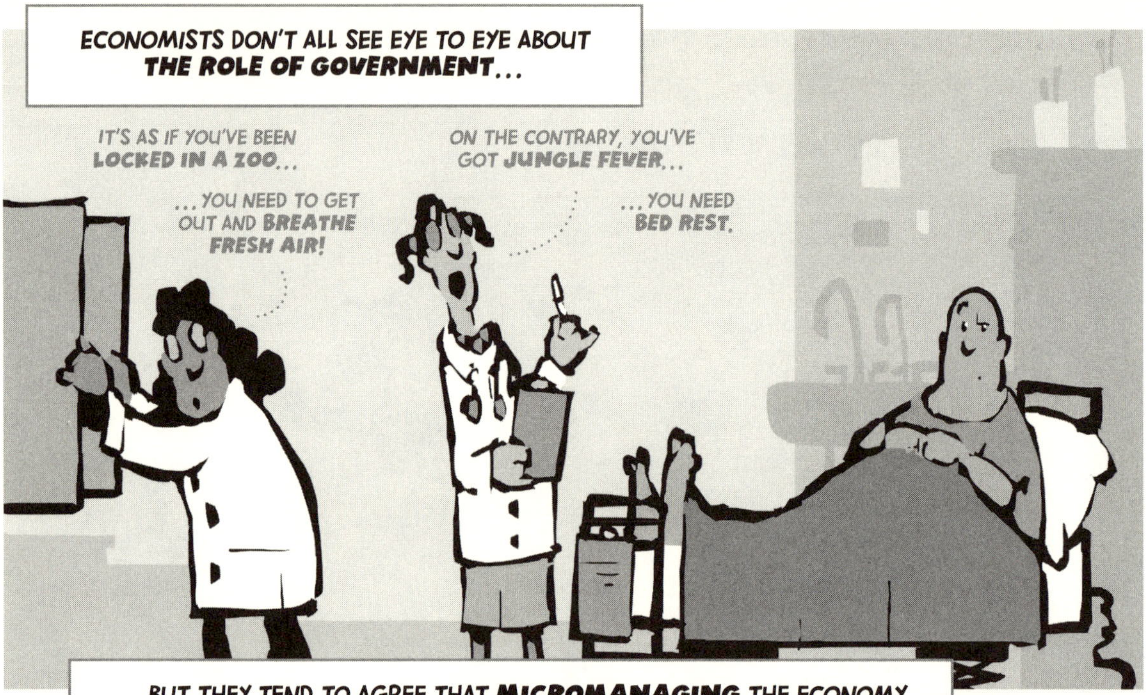

ECONOMISTS DON'T ALL SEE EYE TO EYE ABOUT **THE ROLE OF GOVERNMENT...**

IT'S AS IF YOU'VE BEEN **LOCKED IN A ZOO...**

...YOU NEED TO GET OUT AND **BREATHE FRESH AIR!**

ON THE CONTRARY, YOU'VE GOT **JUNGLE FEVER...**

...YOU NEED **BED REST.**

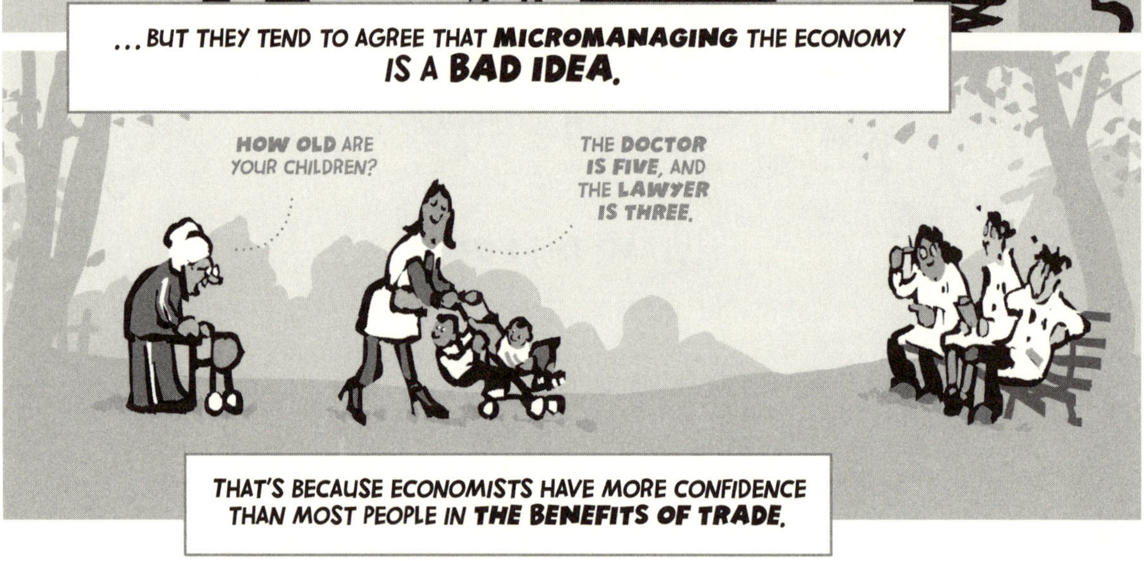

...BUT THEY TEND TO AGREE THAT **MICROMANAGING** THE ECONOMY IS A **BAD IDEA.**

HOW OLD ARE YOUR CHILDREN?

THE **DOCTOR IS FIVE**, AND THE **LAWYER IS THREE.**

THAT'S BECAUSE ECONOMISTS HAVE MORE CONFIDENCE THAN MOST PEOPLE IN **THE BENEFITS OF TRADE.**

PART TWO
INTERNATIONAL TRADE

CHAPTER 7
TRADE AND TECHNOLOGY

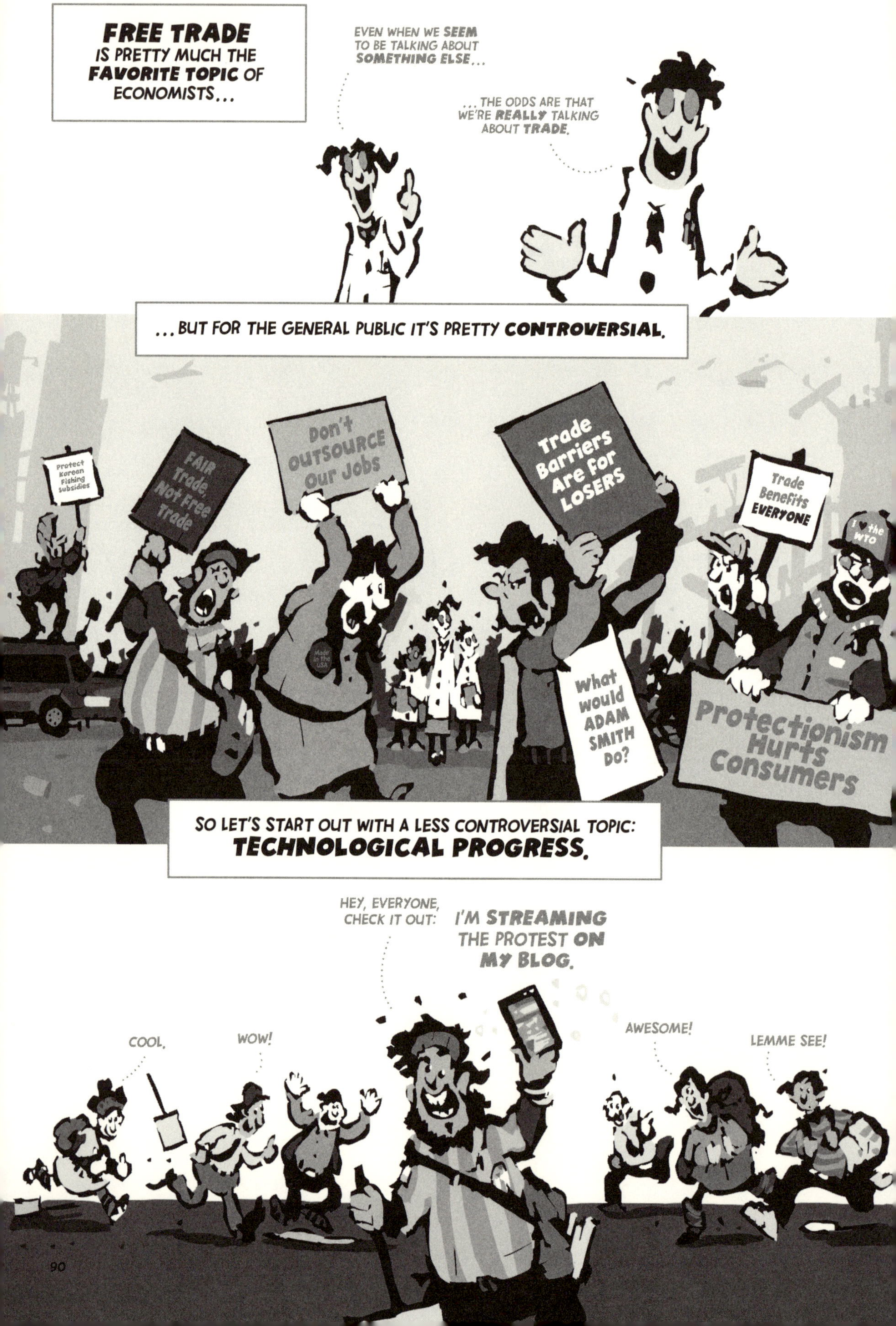

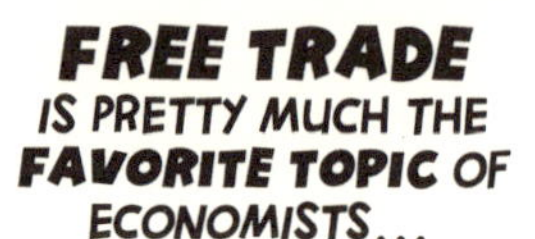

...BUT FOR THE GENERAL PUBLIC IT'S PRETTY **CONTROVERSIAL.**

SO LET'S START OUT WITH A LESS CONTROVERSIAL TOPIC: **TECHNOLOGICAL PROGRESS.**

FOR ECONOMISTS, **TECHNOLOGY** REFERS TO THE WAY **INPUTS** GET TURNED INTO **OUTPUTS**...

...AND **TECHNOLOGICAL PROGRESS** REFERS TO **IMPROVEMENTS IN THAT PROCESS.**

FACT #1:

IT'S TEMPTING TO THINK OF TECHNOLOGICAL PROGRESS AS A KIND OF **MIRACLE THAT BENEFITS EVERYONE**...

WE'RE IN THE MONEY...

...BUT HISTORY SHOWS THAT THIS VIEW IS **OVERLY SIMPLISTIC.**

FOR EXAMPLE, SHIPPING GOODS IN **CONTAINERS** WAS **REVOLUTIONARY**...

...BUT IT DESTROYED THE LIVELIHOODS OF THOUSANDS OF **DOCKWORKERS.**

SIMILARLY, THE **INTERNET** ALLOWED PEOPLE TO BUY THEIR OWN AIRPLANE TICKETS...

...BUT THAT RUINED BUSINESS FOR **TRAVEL AGENTS.**

IN SHORT, TECHNOLOGICAL PROGRESS CAN BE **PAINFUL.**

IF YOU REMEMBER SOME **JARGON FROM MICROECONOMICS**...

...WHAT THIS MEANS IS THAT TECHNOLOGICAL PROGRESS DOES **NOT** USUALLY LEAD TO **PARETO IMPROVEMENTS**.

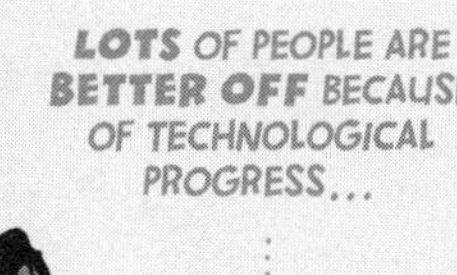

OF COURSE, THIS DOESN'T MEAN TECHNOLOGICAL PROGRESS IS **BAD**.

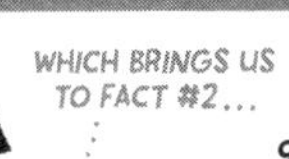

FACT #2: TECHNOLOGICAL PROGRESS IS PRETTY AWESOME.

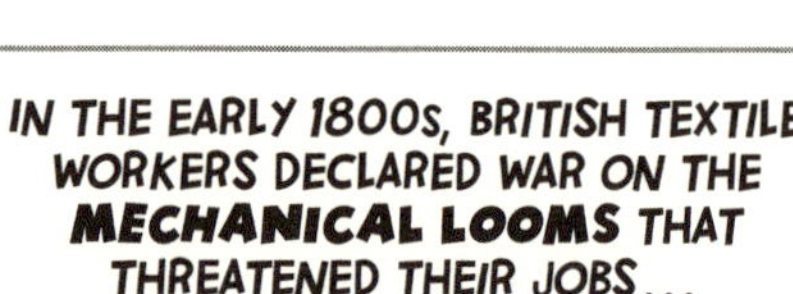

TECHNOLOGICAL PROGRESS IS AWESOME BECAUSE IT ALLOWS US TO GENERATE **MORE OUTPUTS** FROM THE **SAME AMOUNT OF INPUTS.**

AS A RESULT, OVER TIME WE'VE BEEN ABLE TO PRODUCE **MORE OF EVERYTHING FOR EVERYBODY.**

SO EVEN THOUGH IN THE **SHORT RUN** TECHNOLOGICAL PROGRESS CREATES **LOSERS** AS WELL AS **WINNERS**...

...IN THE **LONG RUN** JUST ABOUT **EVERYBODY** IS LIKELY TO BE **BETTER OFF.**

FACT #3: TECHNOLOGICAL PROGRESS AND TRADE ARE ESSENTIALLY INDISTINGUISHABLE.

WHAT THIS MEANS IS THAT **FOR ANY STORY** ABOUT **TECHNOLOGICAL PROGRESS**...

...THERE IS A **SIMILAR STORY** ABOUT **TRADE**...

...AND FOR ANY STORY ABOUT **TRADE**...

...THERE IS, AT LEAST IN THEORY, A **SIMILAR STORY** ABOUT **TECHNOLOGICAL PROGRESS.**

BECAUSE OF FACT #3, YOU SHOULD THINK OF TRADE AND TECHNOLOGICAL PROGRESS AS **IDENTICAL TWINS.**

LIKE TECHNOLOGICAL PROGRESS, TRADE HELPS US GENERATE **MORE OUTPUTS** FROM THE **SAME AMOUNT OF INPUTS.**

OUR **FIRST TWO FACTS** ABOUT TECHNOLOGICAL PROGRESS THEREFORE LEAD TO **TWO IDENTICAL FACTS ABOUT TRADE:**

FACT #1: **TRADE** CREATES **LOSERS** AS WELL AS **WINNERS.**

FACT #2: **TRADE IS PRETTY AWESOME.**

A LOT OF THE CONTROVERSIES ABOUT **FREE TRADE** STEM FROM PEOPLE **FORGETTING** FACT #1 OR FACT #2.

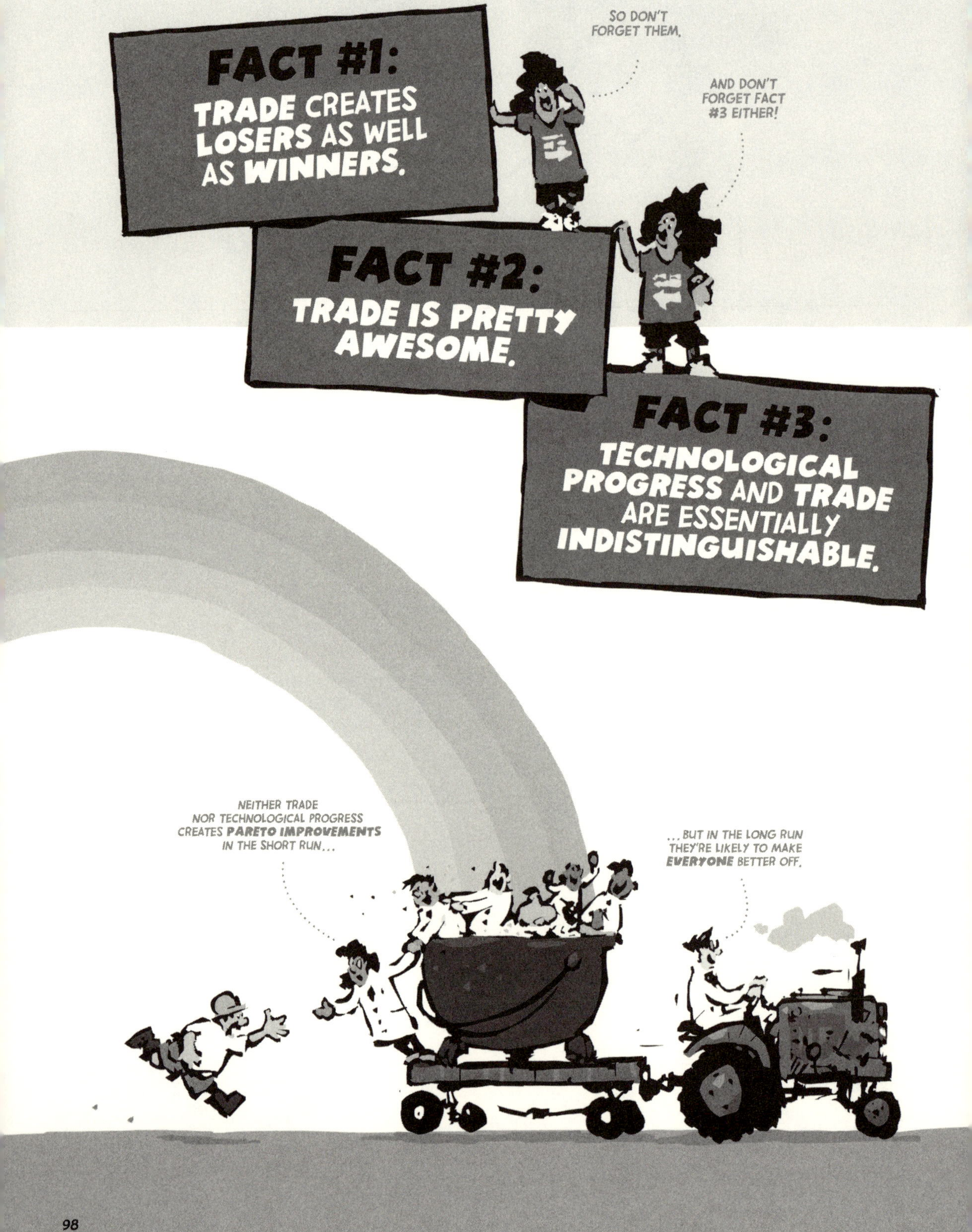

FACT #1:
TRADE CREATES **LOSERS** AS WELL AS **WINNERS.**

SO DON'T FORGET THEM.

AND DON'T FORGET FACT #3 EITHER!

FACT #2:
TRADE IS PRETTY AWESOME.

FACT #3:
TECHNOLOGICAL PROGRESS AND **TRADE** ARE ESSENTIALLY **INDISTINGUISHABLE.**

CHAPTER 8
THE CLASSICAL VIEW OF TRADE

THE WAY THAT **CLASSICAL ECONOMISTS LIKE ADAM SMITH** LOOK AT INTERNATIONAL TRADE IS **SIMPLE AND POWERFUL**...

...AND COMES DIRECTLY FROM THE VIEW THAT THE MACROECONOMY IS LIKE A **WELL-ORGANIZED FAMILY**.

ALTHOUGH TRADE CREATES **LOSERS** AS WELL AS **WINNERS**, CLASSICAL ECONOMISTS FOCUS ON THE **GAINS TO SOCIETY AS A WHOLE**.

CLASSICAL ECONOMISTS ALSO EMPHASIZE THAT TRADE BETWEEN TWO COUNTRIES CAN BENEFIT **BOTH COUNTRIES.**

IN 1817 **DAVID RICARDO'S** THEORY OF **COMPARATIVE ADVANTAGE** SHOWED THAT THESE **MUTUAL BENEFITS** ARE POSSIBLE WHEN COUNTRIES ARE **DIFFERENT...**

...BUT MODERN ECONOMISTS BELIEVE THAT MUTUAL BENEFITS ARE POSSIBLE EVEN WHEN COUNTRIES ARE **SIMILAR.**

PAUL KRUGMAN WON THE 2008 NOBEL PRIZE FOR HIS WORK IN THIS AREA.

THE **BENEFITS OF TRADE** ARE MOST OBVIOUS WHEN YOU THINK ABOUT **FAMILIES** TRADING WITH **OTHER FAMILIES**...
WITHOUT YOU, MRS. TAYLOR, MY LIFE WOULD BE **THREADBARE!**
OH, **BLESS YOUR SOUL**, MR. SHOEMAKER.
...BUT YOU CAN ALSO EASILY SEE THE BENEFITS OF TRADING WITH **OTHER COUNTRIES**...

LOOK, HERE COMES MONSIEUR **CHAPEAU!**
WITHOUT THE FRENCH, I DON'T KNOW HOW WE'D GET **AHEAD**.

...OR EVEN
WITH **ALIENS.**
TAKE ME TO YOUR
LEADING ECONOMIST.

YOU MIGHT NOT THINK THAT ADAM SMITH WOULD HAVE MUCH TO SAY ABOUT ALIENS...
LIFE ON OTHER PLANETS?
I'M STILL GETTING USED TO THE IDEA OF LIFE IN SOUTH AMERICA.

...BUT IN FACT CLASSICAL ECONOMICS TEACHES US AN IMPORTANT LESSON ABOUT INTERSTELLAR TRADE:
IF WE ENCOUNTER BEINGS FROM ANOTHER PLANET...
OR IF THEY ENCOUNTER US!

...AND IF BOTH SIDES ENGAGE PEACEFULLY IN FREE TRADE...
WANT THIS CANDY BAR?
THEN YOU HAVE TO TRADE ME FOR IT...
...AND NO BULLYING!

...THEN THIS ALIEN ENCOUNTER WOULD BE PRETTY AWESOME FOR BOTH SIDES.
I'M BETTER OFF, AND SO IS MY NEW FRIEND ZANTROK!
ZEEKROX FLOUDZ, HOOGHA HOO GHOW ZGR STEVE!

WE EARTHLINGS WOULD BENEFIT REGARDLESS OF WHETHER THE ALIENS WERE **LESS ADVANCED** THAN US...
NEED A **HAND** WITH THAT?
LIFE WAS MUCH HARDER BEFORE WE HUMANS DISCOVERED THE PLANET GXHSNAEL!
...OR **MORE ADVANCED.**
CANCER? HECK, WE CURED THAT **EONS AGO.**
LIFE WAS MUCH HARDER BEFORE THE GXHSNAELIANS DISCOVERED PLANET EARTH!
PLUS THERE WOULD BE ADDED BENEFITS FROM **SHARING NEW VARIETIES OF FOOD AND ARTS.**
CAN YOU BELIEVE THAT THE PRICE OF ADMISSION IS JUST **ONE AVOCADO?**
WHAT'S AN AVOCADO?

OF COURSE, THERE WOULD BE A DOWNSIDE: INTERSTELLAR TRADE WOULD CREATE **LOSERS** AS WELL AS **WINNERS.**

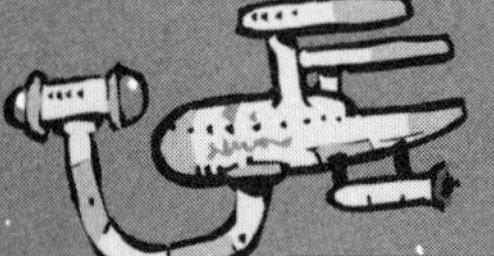

BUT CLASSICAL ECONOMISTS RESPOND TO CONCERNS ABOUT **OUTSOURCING**...

...BY POINTING OUT THAT **FAMILIES** ENGAGE IN OUTSOURCING TOO.

WHETHER YOU'RE A FAMILY, A COUNTRY, OR A PLANET,
OUTSOURCING ALLOWS YOU TO FOCUS ON WHAT YOU'RE GOOD AT.

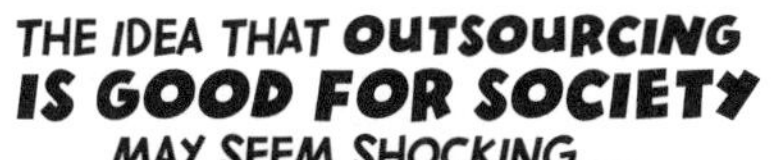

THE IDEA THAT **OUTSOURCING IS GOOD FOR SOCIETY** MAY SEEM SHOCKING...

...BUT REMEMBER THAT CLASSICAL ECONOMISTS VIEW THE ECONOMY AS **A FINELY TUNED JOB-CREATING MACHINE.**

THIS ALSO EXPLAINS WHY CLASSICAL ECONOMISTS BELIEVE THAT THE BEST THING ABOUT TRADE ISN'T **EXPORTING**...

...BUT **IMPORTING.**

AS ALWAYS, THIS CLASSICAL VIEW PARALLELS THE PERSPECTIVE OF A **WELL-ORGANIZED FAMILY.**

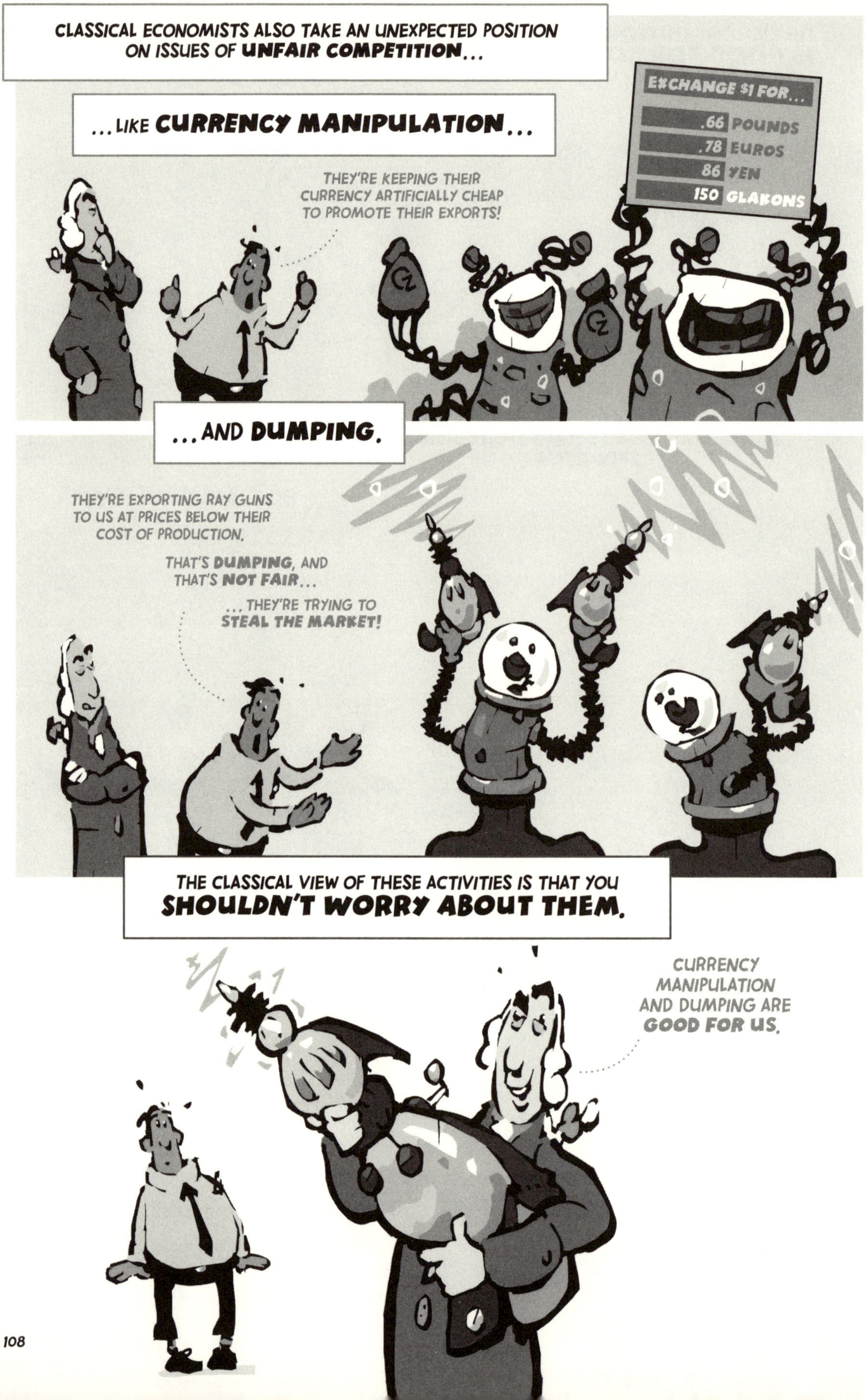

CLASSICAL ECONOMISTS ALSO TAKE AN UNEXPECTED POSITION ON ISSUES OF **UNFAIR COMPETITION**...

...LIKE **CURRENCY MANIPULATION**...

...AND **DUMPING.**

THE CLASSICAL VIEW OF THESE ACTIVITIES IS THAT YOU **SHOULDN'T WORRY ABOUT THEM.**

AS WITH OUTSOURCING, THIS CLASSICAL VIEW IS DRIVEN BY A **CONFIDENT ATTITUDE ABOUT JOB CREATION**...

...AND BY A FOCUS ON **IMPORTS**, NOT **EXPORTS**.

AND ONCE AGAIN THERE IS A PARALLEL WITH **FAMILIES**.

AS WE'LL SEE IN THE NEXT CHAPTER, THIS CLASSICAL PERSPECTIVE CAN BE **A LITTLE SIMPLISTIC.**

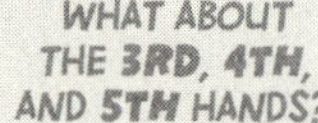

NONETHELESS, CLASSICAL ECONOMICS CONTRIBUTES VALUABLE IDEAS TO DISCUSSIONS OF FREE TRADE, WHETHER IT'S WITH A NEIGHBORING **PLANET**...

...OR WITH A NEIGHBORING **HOUSEHOLD** OR **COUNTRY**.

CHAPTER 9
COMPLICATIONS

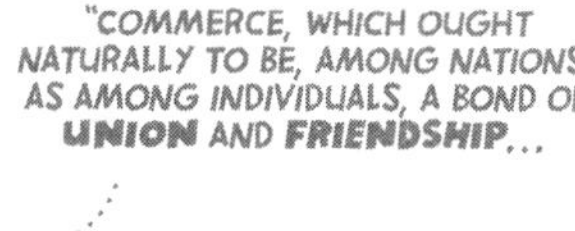

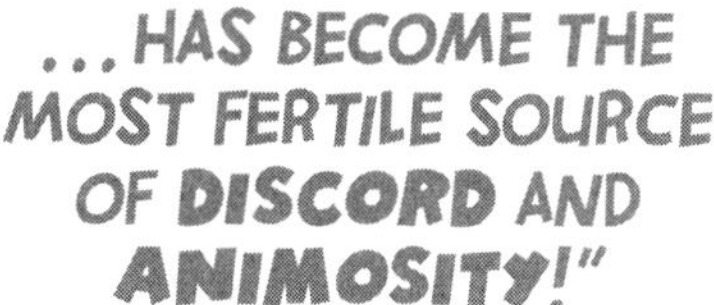

THE RESULTING CONCLUSIONS ABOUT **TRADE** SEEM SO COMPELLING...

...THAT IT'S A BIT OF A SHOCK TO ENCOUNTER **COMPLICATIONS** RELATED TO **HUMAN RIGHTS**...

...AND THE **ENVIRONMENT**...

...AND **INFANT INDUSTRIES**.

GREAT, NOW GET OUT THERE AND **COMPETE!**

AND OF COURSE THERE ARE **SHORT-RUN COMPLICATIONS** RELATING TO THE **BUSINESS CYCLE**.

THESE COMPLICATIONS **CANNOT BE EASILY DISMISSED.**

THE CLASSICAL PERSPECTIVE PROMISES THAT TRADE BETWEEN COUNTRIES BENEFITS **BOTH** COUNTRIES...

...AND TRADE THAT MIGHT HURT **BOTH** COUNTRIES.

BECAUSE OF GLOBAL WARMING, TRADE COULD MAKE **EVERYONE** WORSE OFF.

WE'LL COME BACK TO THIS IN CHAPTER 14.

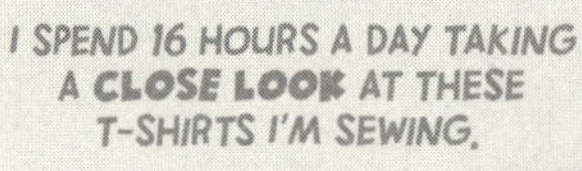

SWEATSHOP LABOR CAN OF COURSE PROVIDE **BENEFITS** FOR **MANUFACTURERS** AND **THEIR CUSTOMERS**...

...BUT MANY PEOPLE THINK OF IT AS **EXPLOITATION**, LIKE **SLAVERY**.

UNLIKE **SLAVERY**, HOWEVER, MANY SWEATSHOPS DON'T INVOLVE **EXPLOITATION BY FORCE**...

...BUT RATHER, **EXPLOITATION BY CHOICE.**

OPPONENTS OF SWEATSHOPS POINT OUT THAT SIMILAR WORKING CONDITIONS USED TO EXIST IN THE U.S. AND OTHER RICH COUNTRIES...

...BUT WE **PASSED LAWS BANNING THESE PRACTICES.**

AND IF SWEATSHOPS ARE **ILLEGAL** IN **RICH COUNTRIES**...

...HOW CAN IT BE **OKAY** TO HAVE THEM IN **POOR COUNTRIES** THAT SELL TO US?

ANTI-SWEATSHOP ACTIVISTS ARGUE THAT WE NEED TO PROTECT THE **HEALTH AND SAFETY** OF **ALL** WORKERS.

THEY WARN THAT THE ALTERNATIVE IS A **SLIPPERY SLOPE**...

... THAT COULD ULTIMATELY THREATEN WORKING STANDARDS **EVERYWHERE**.

SUPPORTERS OF SWEATSHOPS RESPOND THAT "EXPLOITATION" MAY BE THE BEST AVAILABLE OPTION FOR MANY PEOPLE.
WHAT IF THE ONLY THING WORSE THAN BEING EXPLOITED...
...IS NOT BEING EXPLOITED?
Will Work For Food

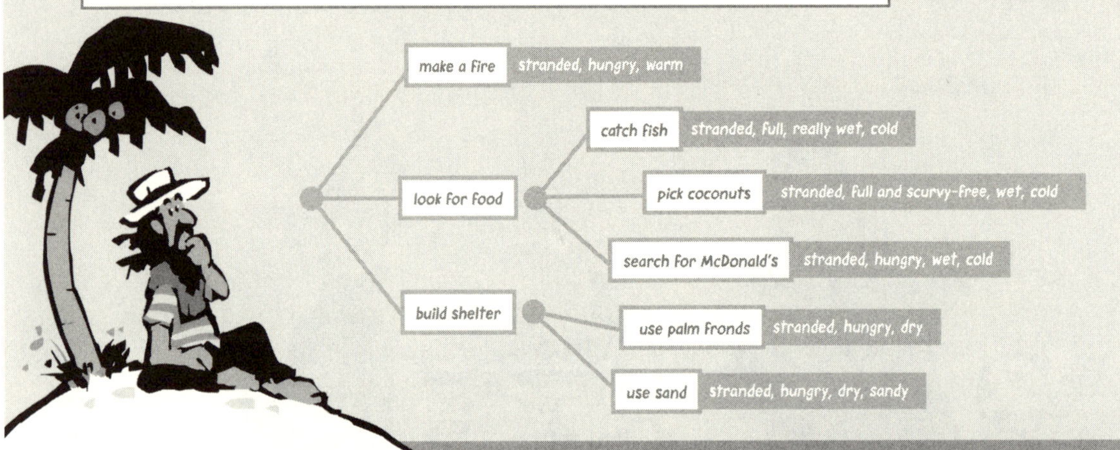
IN MICROECONOMICS WE LEARNED THAT OPTIMIZING INDIVIDUALS LOOK AT THEIR OPTIONS AND CHOOSE THE BEST ONE.
make a fire
stranded, hungry, warm
look for food
catch fish
stranded, full, really wet, cold
pick coconuts
stranded, full and scurvy-free, wet, cold
search for McDonald's
stranded, hungry, wet, cold
build shelter
use palm fronds
stranded, hungry, dry
use sand
stranded, hungry, dry, sandy

SO IF WORKING IN A SWEATSHOP IS THE OPTION SOMEONE CHOOSES...
...THEN THE OTHER OPTIONS MUST HAVE BEEN EVEN WORSE.
Will Work For Food

THE SAD TRUTH ABOUT THE WORLD IS THAT MANY PEOPLE LIVE IN **GRINDING POVERTY**...

...AND IN COMPARISON SWEATSHOP JOBS CAN SEEM **TERRIFIC.**

THAT'S WHY SOME STAUNCH ANTI-POVERTY ACTIVISTS **DEFEND SWEATSHOPS.**

IN THE END, THE QUESTION OF WHETHER SWEATSHOPS ARE GOOD OR BAD IS **TRICKY.**

MAKING MATTERS EVEN TRICKIER IS THE PROBLEM OF
THE WOLF IN SHEEP'S CLOTHING.

IN OTHER WORDS, SOME OF THE OPPOSITION TO HAVING SWEATSHOPS IN **POOR COUNTRIES**...

...COMES FROM MEMBERS OF **RICH COUNTRIES** WHOSE
TRUE CONCERN IS FOR THEIR OWN JOBS AND PROFITS.

THE WOLF-IN-SHEEP'S-CLOTHING PROBLEM BEDEVILS **ALL ARGUMENTS ABOUT FREE TRADE.**

THE FACT IS THAT SOME BUSINESSES AND WORKERS **IN RICH COUNTRIES** WILL SAY ANYTHING TO **AVOID COMPETITION FROM POOR COUNTRIES...**

...AND SOME BUSINESSES AND WORKERS **IN POOR COUNTRIES** WILL SAY ANYTHING TO **AVOID COMPETITION FROM RICH COUNTRIES.**

THESE ARGUMENTS ARE MADE OUT OF **NARROW SELF-INTEREST,** WHICH MAY NOT MATCH UP WITH THE **GENERAL WELFARE.**

OVERALL, THE CASE FOR FREE TRADE IS NOT THE **100% SLAM DUNK** THAT CLASSICAL ECONOMISTS MAKE IT OUT TO BE...

...AND IT'S DEFINITELY TRUE THAT THERE ARE **OTHER THINGS** THAT FOLKS IN RICH COUNTRIES CAN DO TO HELP FOLKS IN POOR COUNTRIES.

BUT MOST ECONOMISTS ARGUE THAT THE **BURDEN OF PROOF** IN THE DEBATE ABOUT FREE TRADE **LIES WITH THOSE WHO OPPOSE IT.**

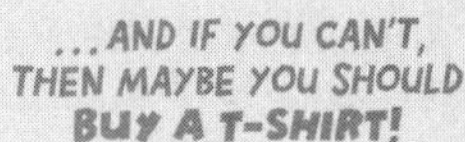

CHAPTER 10
FOREIGN AID

THAT'S THE **MIRACLE** OF ADAM SMITH'S INVISIBLE HAND.

UNFORTUNATELY, **WORLD HISTORY** HASN'T EXACTLY **FOLLOWED ADAM SMITH'S VISION OF FREE TRADE**...

...AND THAT'S JUST ONE REASON WHY SOME PEOPLE **WANT TO DO MORE** TO HELP POOR COUNTRIES.

THE **FIRST IMPORTANT LESSON** FOR THOSE WHO WANT TO HELP...

ONE GOOD EXAMPLE INVOLVES **NATURAL RESOURCES** LIKE **FISHERIES.**

FISHERIES ARE A CLASSIC **TRAGEDY OF THE COMMONS**. . .

. . . AND ECONOMISTS USED TO THINK THEY KNEW **EVERYTHING** ABOUT HOW TO RESPOND.

BUT IT TURNS OUT THAT THE TRAGEDY OF THE COMMONS IS **NOT INEVITABLE.**

IN SOME PARTS OF THE WORLD, **LOCAL COMMUNITIES** HAVE MANAGED TO PROTECT THEIR OWN FISHERIES.

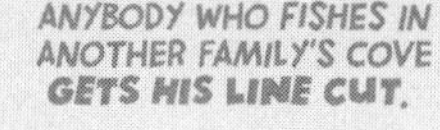

ELINOR OSTROM SHARED THE NOBEL PRIZE IN 2009 FOR STUDYING THESE **BRILLIANT HOMEGROWN SOLUTIONS.**

HER RESEARCH HELPS EXPLAIN WHY FOREIGN AID IS SUCH **A DELICATE BALANCING ACT.**

GIVEN THE CHALLENGES OF HELPING A **STRUGGLING FAMILY**...

...IT'S NO SURPRISE THAT HELPING A **STRUGGLING ECONOMY** IS ALSO HARD.

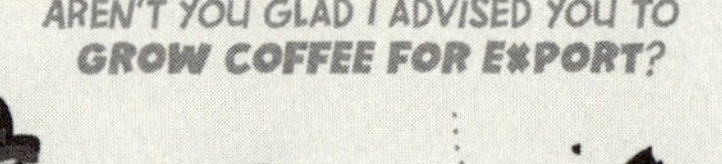

IN PART THIS IS BECAUSE OF THE **VARIETY OF PROBLEMS** THAT CAN HAMPER REFORM EFFORTS.

OF COURSE, IT'S ALSO POSSIBLE TO BE TOO CAUTIOUS.
HELP!
OUR HOUSE IS BURNING DOWN!
AND LOCUSTS ARE EATING ALL OF OUR CROPS!
AND MEN WITH GUNS STOLE ALL OUR MONEY!
SORRY, WE CAN'T HELP.
WE'RE TRYING TO BE HUMBLE.
Humility

THE DELICATE BALANCING ACT OF FOREIGN AID IS EVEN EVIDENT IN PROGRAMS LIKE **MICROFINANCE**...

...WHICH THE ECONOMIST **MUHAMMAD YUNUS** STARTED IN HIS NATIVE BANGLADESH.

THE SUCCESS OF MICROFINANCE WON YUNUS AND HIS **GRAMEEN BANK** THE 2006 NOBEL PEACE PRIZE...

...BUT WHEN IT COMES TO FOREIGN AID, **CONTROVERSY IS NEVER FAR BEHIND.**

PERHAPS THE **MOST CONTROVERSIAL** ASPECT OF FOREIGN AID IS **CONDITIONALITY.**

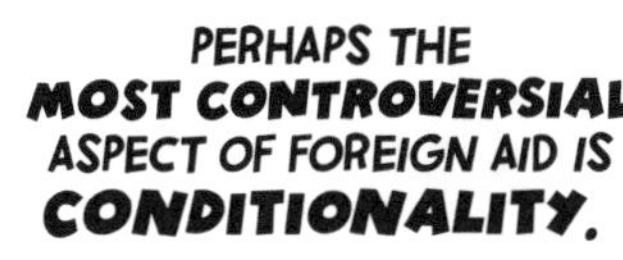

ON THE ONE HAND, **CONDITIONAL AID** PROGRAMS **DON'T INVOLVE MUCH HUMILITY...**

...ESPECIALLY COMPARED WITH **UNCONDITIONAL AID,** LIKE **MEDICAL CARE.**

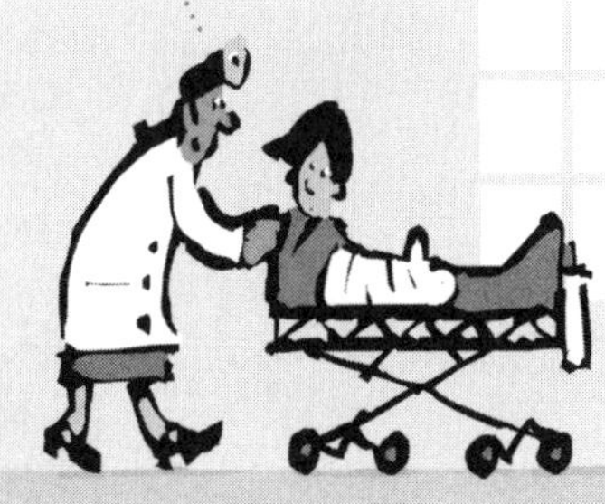

ON THE OTHER HAND, WEALTHY FOREIGN COUNTRIES AND INTERNATIONAL INSTITUTIONS...

...ARE UNLIKELY TO JUST GIVE AWAY MONEY **WITH NO STRINGS ATTACHED.**

DEVELOPMENT ECONOMISTS WORK HARD TO MANAGE ALL THESE CHALLENGES AND IMPROVE FOREIGN AID.

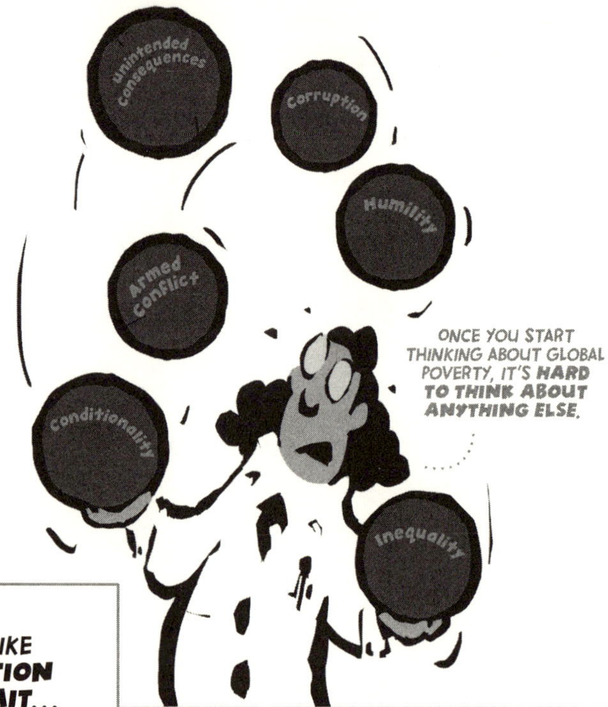

ECONOMIC RESEARCH RANGES FROM EXPERIMENTS RUN BY GROUPS LIKE **INNOVATIONS FOR POVERTY ACTION** AND THE **POVERTY ACTION LAB** AT **MIT**...

...TO STUDIES OF HOMEGROWN ANTIPOVERTY PROGRAMS LIKE MEXICO'S **OPORTUNIDADES.**

ECONOMISTS CAN ALSO HELP BY ANALYZING THE BARRIERS TO ECONOMIC GROWTH...
MALARIA AND PNEUMOCOCCAL DISEASES KILL MILLIONS OF PEOPLE...
...BUT BECAUSE THOSE DEATHS MOSTLY OCCUR IN POOR COUNTRIES...
...THERE'S NO FINANCIAL INCENTIVE FOR DRUG COMPANIES TO DEVELOP A VACCINE.
...AND CREATING INNOVATIVE WAYS TO OVERCOME THOSE BARRIERS.
RICH COUNTRIES AND FOUNDATIONS ARE OFFERING A $1.5 BILLION PRIZE FOR VACCINE DEVELOPMENT!
FINALLY, ECONOMISTS CAN HELP BY ADVISING POOR COUNTRIES ABOUT MACROECONOMIC POLICY...
IF YOU PRINT TOO MUCH MONEY, YOU'RE JUST GOING TO GET INFLATION.
...AND BY ADVISING RICH COUNTRIES ABOUT THE BEST WAYS TO PROVIDE FOREIGN AID.
HOW CAN WE HELP THEM GET THEIR ACT TOGETHER?
WE'RE GLAD YOU ASKED! A GOOD FIRST STEP...
...IS FOR YOU TO GET YOUR ACT TOGETHER.
LET'S SEE WHY...

WHEN IT COMES TO FOREIGN AID, MANY ECONOMISTS **OBSESS** ABOUT GETTING **RICH COUNTRIES TO REDUCE THEIR TRADE BARRIERS.**

THIS IS ESPECIALLY TRUE IN **AGRICULTURE**, AN AREA WHERE POOR COUNTRIES OFTEN HAVE A **COMPARATIVE ADVANTAGE.**

UNFORTUNATELY, MANY RICH COUNTRIES ENGAGE IN **PROTECTIONISM**...

...AND PROVIDE **SUBSIDIES TO THEIR OWN PRODUCERS.**

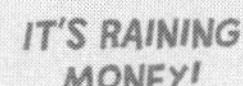

...BUT TRADE BARRIERS **HURT RICH-COUNTRY CONSUMERS**...

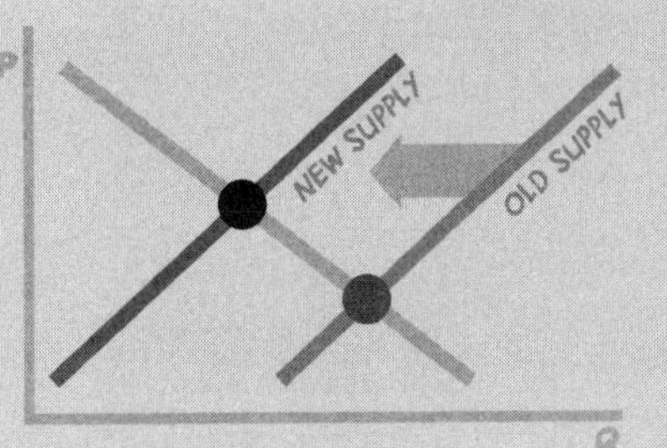

...AND SUBSIDIES **HURT RICH-COUNTRY TAXPAYERS.**

PERHAPS WORST OF ALL, THESE POLICIES
HURT FARMERS IN POOR COUNTRIES.

WHEN YOU CONSIDER THAT WHAT RICH-WORLD GOVERNMENTS SPEND **ON THEIR OWN FARMERS...**

...IS ON AVERAGE **4 TIMES LARGER** THAN WHAT THEY SPEND ON **FOREIGN AID...**

...IT'S NO WONDER THAT MANY ECONOMISTS BELIEVE THAT **ONE OF THE BEST FORMS OF AID IS TRADE.**

IF YOU WANT TO HELP POOR COUNTRIES...

...MAKE IT EASY TO BUY STUFF FROM THEM!

CHAPTER 11
FOREIGN CURRENCIES

DIFFERENT COUNTRIES USE **DIFFERENT CURRENCIES.**

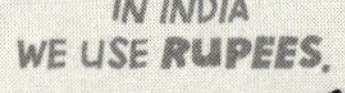

THIS CAN COMPLICATE **INTERNATIONAL TRADE...**

...BUT THERE'S A **SOLUTION.**

THE **FOREIGN EXCHANGE MARKET** IS WHERE PEOPLE **TRADE ONE CURRENCY** FOR **ANOTHER.**

IN MANY WAYS, THE FOREIGN EXCHANGE MARKET IS **JUST LIKE ANY OTHER MARKET**...

...IT'S ALL **SUPPLY AND DEMAND!**

FOR EXAMPLE, SOME PEOPLE WANT TO TRADE **DOLLARS** FOR **RUPEES**...

...AND SOME PEOPLE WANT TO TRADE **RUPEES** FOR **DOLLARS**...

...AND THE RESULT IS AN **EXCHANGE RATE**.

EXCHANGE RATES ARE CALLED **FLOATING** OR **FLEXIBLE** WHEN THEY FLUCTUATE BASED ON MARKET SUPPLY AND DEMAND.

IT'S TEMPTING TO THINK THAT IT'S **GOOD** WHEN YOUR CURRENCY GETS **STRONGER**...

...AND **BAD** WHEN YOUR CURRENCY GETS **WEAKER**...

...BUT THE TRUTH IS THAT EXCHANGE RATE FLUCTUATIONS PRODUCE BOTH **WINNERS AND LOSERS.**

EXCHANGE RATE FLUCTUATIONS HAVE DIFFERENT EFFECTS ON **EXPORTERS...**

...AND **IMPORTERS.**

THIS IS LIKE THE WAY **FLUCTUATING RATES OF INFLATION** HAVE DIFFERENT EFFECTS ON **BORROWERS...**

...AND **LENDERS.**

AS WITH INFLATION, HOWEVER, TOO MUCH **CONFUSION AND UNCERTAINTY** CAN BE **BAD FOR EVERYONE.**

ONE WAY TO AVOID CONFUSION AND UNCERTAINTY IS TO HAVE **FIXED EXCHANGE RATES...**

...BUT THAT REQUIRES **GOVERNMENT INTERVENTION.**

JUST LIKE A CENTRAL BANK CAN BUY AND SELL **ASSETS** TO INFLUENCE **INTEREST RATES...**

...A CENTRAL BANK CAN BUY AND SELL **FOREIGN CURRENCY** TO INFLUENCE **EXCHANGE RATES.**

FOR EXAMPLE, UNTIL 1994 **MEXICO** PEGGED ITS **PESO** TO THE **U.S. DOLLAR.**

UNFORTUNATELY, IT CAN BE **HARD TO KEEP FIXED EXCHANGE RATES FIXED.**

IN 1994 LOTS OF PEOPLE WANTED TO **SELL MEXICAN PESOS** AND **BUY U.S. DOLLARS...**

...SO IN ORDER TO MAINTAIN A FIXED EXCHANGE RATE, THE MEXICAN GOVERNMENT HAD TO **DO THE OPPOSITE.**

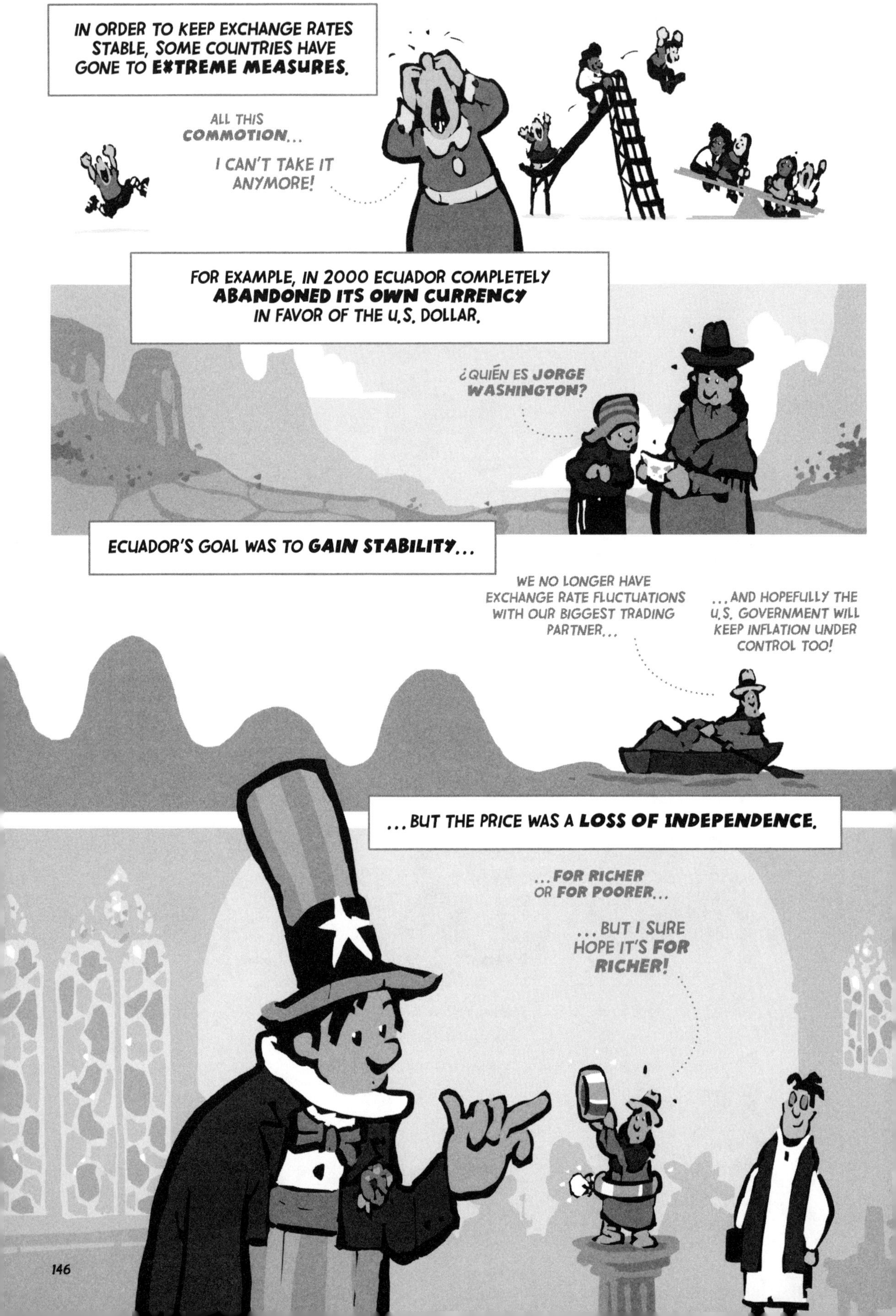

IN ORDER TO KEEP EXCHANGE RATES STABLE, SOME COUNTRIES HAVE GONE TO **EXTREME MEASURES.**

FOR EXAMPLE, IN 2000 ECUADOR COMPLETELY **ABANDONED ITS OWN CURRENCY** IN FAVOR OF THE U.S. DOLLAR.

ECUADOR'S GOAL WAS TO **GAIN STABILITY**...

WE NO LONGER HAVE EXCHANGE RATE FLUCTUATIONS WITH OUR BIGGEST TRADING PARTNER...

...AND HOPEFULLY THE U.S. GOVERNMENT WILL KEEP INFLATION UNDER CONTROL TOO!

...BUT THE PRICE WAS A **LOSS OF INDEPENDENCE.**

...**FOR RICHER** OR **FOR POORER**...

...BUT I SURE HOPE IT'S **FOR RICHER!**

ANOTHER EXTREME EXAMPLE FEATURES THE EUROPEAN COUNTRIES THAT **JOINED TOGETHER** IN 1999...

...TO ADOPT A **SINGLE CURRENCY**.

ONCE AGAIN, THE BENEFIT WAS **ELIMINATING** THE DIFFICULTIES ASSOCIATED WITH HAVING MULTIPLE CURRENCIES...

...AND ONCE AGAIN THE COST WAS A **LOSS OF INDEPENDENCE** FOR THESE EUROPEAN ECONOMIES.

IT CAN BE HARD TO WEIGH THE **COSTS AND BENEFITS** OF A **CURRENCY UNION**...

IT'S NO SURPRISE THAT MUNDELL'S WORK HIGHLIGHTS THE IMPORTANCE OF **TOGETHERNESS**...

...BUT IT ALSO HIGHLIGHTS THE IMPORTANCE OF **LABOR AND CAPITAL MOBILITY**.

THE BIGGEST SURPRISE IN MUNDELL'S WORK CONCERNS A TRIO KNOWN AS THE **IMPOSSIBLE TRINITY:**

FREELY TRADED CURRENCY

INDEPENDENT MONETARY POLICY

FIXED EXCHANGE RATES

HAVING ALL THREE **SOUNDS GREAT**, BUT THEY'RE AN IMPOSSIBLE TRINITY BECAUSE YOU CAN ONLY HAVE **TWO OUT OF THREE.**

ULTIMATELY, DIFFERENT COUNTRIES CHOOSE **DIFFERENT COMBINATIONS** OF THE IMPOSSIBLE TRINITY.

WHICH ONES TO CHOOSE IS **NOT AN EASY QUESTION**...

...AND AS WITH MARRIAGE, THERE'S **NOT ALWAYS A RIGHT ANSWER.**

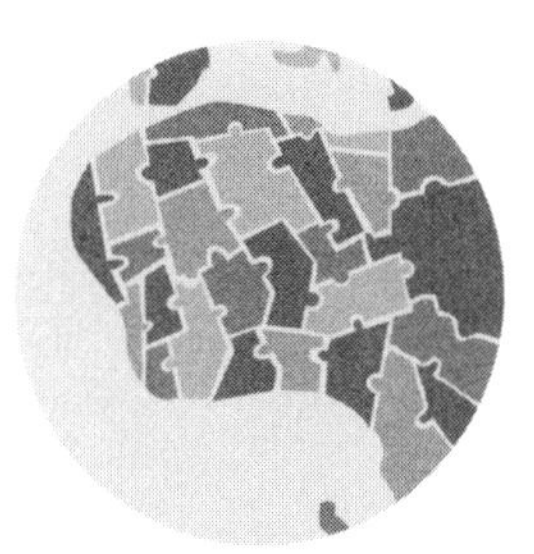

PART THREE
GLOBAL MACROECONOMICS

CHAPTER 12
THE END OF THE BUSINESS CYCLE?

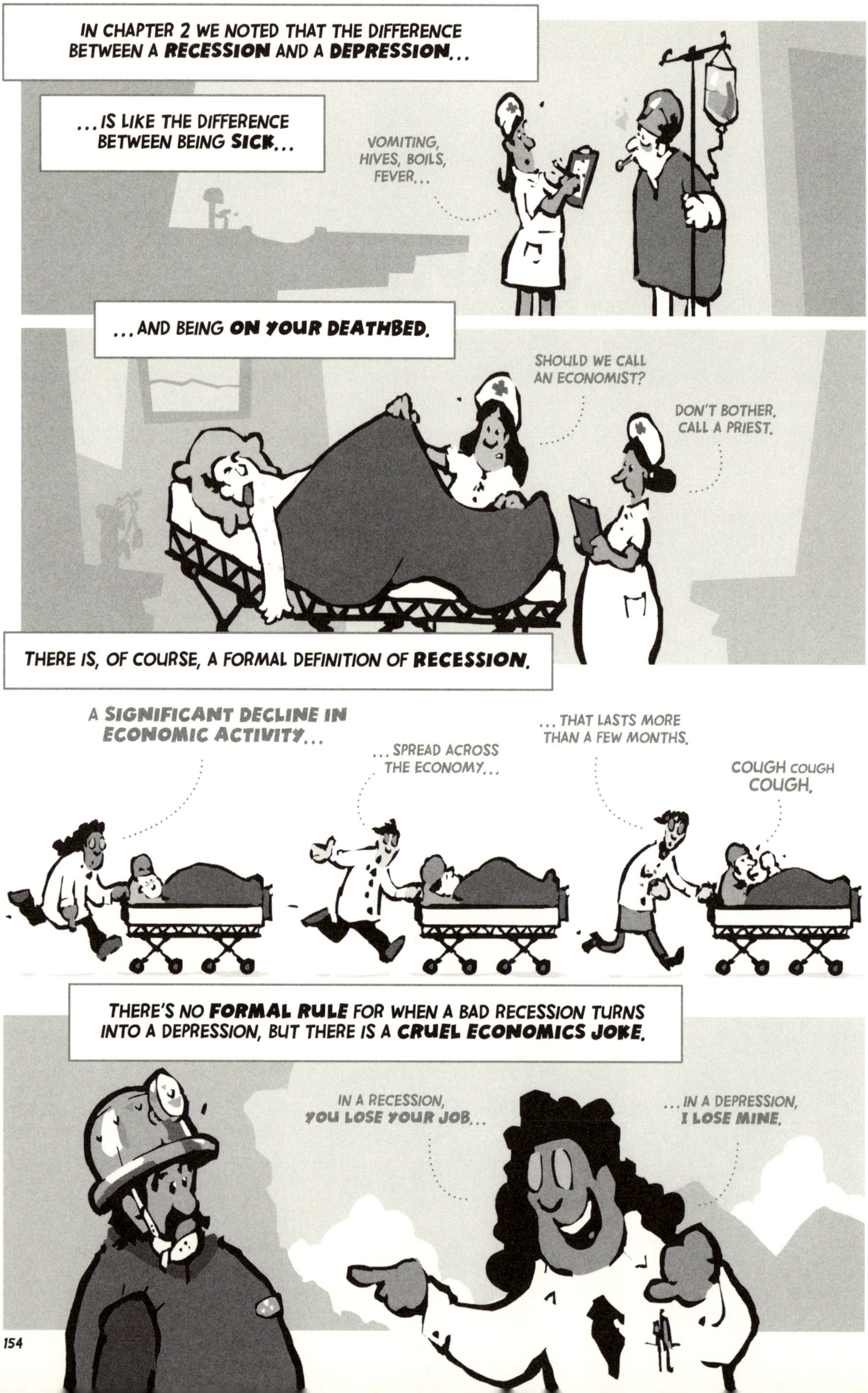

IN CHAPTER 2 WE NOTED THAT THE DIFFERENCE BETWEEN A **RECESSION** AND A **DEPRESSION**...

...IS LIKE THE DIFFERENCE BETWEEN BEING **SICK**...

VOMITING, HIVES, BOILS, FEVER...

...AND BEING **ON YOUR DEATHBED.**

SHOULD WE CALL AN ECONOMIST?

DON'T BOTHER, CALL A PRIEST.

THERE IS, OF COURSE, A FORMAL DEFINITION OF **RECESSION.**

AT THE END OF THE 20TH CENTURY, ECONOMISTS LIKE **ROBERT LUCAS** EXPRESSED GREAT CONFIDENCE THAT **DEPRESSIONS WERE A THING OF THE PAST.**

AND NO WONDER: MORE THAN **TWO DECADES** OF LOW INFLATION, LOW UNEMPLOYMENT, AND RELATIVELY STEADY GROWTH IN THE RICH WORLD...

...MADE IT SEEM AS IF THE **END OF THE BUSINESS CYCLE** WAS **WITHIN REACH.**

THEN CAME THE **FINANCIAL CRISIS** OF 2008...

...AND SUDDENLY THE GREAT DEPRESSION DIDN'T SEEM LIKE **ANCIENT HISTORY.**

THE GREAT DEPRESSION STARTED AFTER A **DECADE OF PROSPERITY** FEATURING SOARING STOCK MARKETS AND HOUSING PRICES IN THE U.S.

THEN, IN 1929, THE **STOCK MARKET CRASHED**...

...A WAVE OF **BANK FAILURES** SWEPT THE COUNTRY...

...NATIONAL ECONOMIES AND INTERNATIONAL TRADE **COLLAPSED**...

...AND **UNEMPLOYMENT SOARED.**

COMPARED TO THE **GREAT DEPRESSION**...
... THE "**GREAT RECESSION**" WAS **NOTHING**.
1929–1933
2007–2009
DECLINE IN U.S. REAL GDP

27%

5%
PEAK U.S. UNEMPLOYMENT
25%

10%
DECLINE IN WORLD TRADE
36%

20%
DURATION OF RECESSION
43 MONTHS WITHOUT ECONOMIC GROWTH.

18 MONTHS? PIECE OF CAKE.

MANY FACTORS CONTRIBUTED TO THE GREAT DEPRESSION...

HYPOTHERMIA, GANGRENE, HYPOXIA, MALNUTRITION...
...BUT AT THE TOP OF THE LIST WAS
BAD MONETARY POLICY BY THE FEDERAL RESERVE.

LET'S OPERATE!

AS WE LEARNED IN CHAPTER 3, THE WAY TO STIMULATE THE ECONOMY IS TO LOOSEN MONETARY POLICY...
I'VE NEVER DONE THIS BEFORE...
...BUT DON'T WORRY!

...BUT THE FED, WHICH HAD BEEN CREATED ONLY A FEW YEARS EARLIER, DID JUST THE OPPOSITE.
YOU MEAN I WASN'T SUPPOSED TO AMPUTATE THE LEFT LEG?
CLASSIC ROOKIE MISTAKE.

IN CONTRAST, THE FED'S RESPONSE TO THE "GREAT RECESSION" WAS TO **TAKE ACTION** TO **STIMULATE BORROWING AND SPENDING...**

...AND IN FACT THE FED LOWERED INTEREST RATES **ALL THE WAY TO ZERO.**

ONE OF THE BIG DEBATES ABOUT THE 2008 CRISIS IS WHETHER THE FED **COULD HAVE DONE EVEN MORE...**

...OR WHETHER MONETARY POLICY HAD **MET ITS MATCH.**

UNFORTUNATELY, DURING THE **GREAT DEPRESSION** THE U.S. GOVERNMENT ALSO **BOTCHED FISCAL POLICY.**

THE ECONOMIC ORTHODOXY IN THOSE DAYS FAVORED **BALANCED BUDGETS...**

...AND THE VIEWS OF **JOHN MAYNARD KEYNES...**

...WERE SEEN AS **HERESY.**

NOWADAYS, THE KEYNESIAN IDEA OF **FISCAL STIMULUS** IS PRETTY **MAINSTREAM**...

...AND THE **STIMULUS BILLS** AND **TAX CUTS OF 2008–2009** WERE RIGHT OUT OF THE **KEYNESIAN PLAYBOOK.**

MOST ECONOMISTS AGREE THAT WITHOUT THESE POLICIES THE 2008 RECESSION WOULD HAVE BEEN **EVEN WORSE**...

...JUST LIKE MANY ECONOMISTS THINK THAT **MASSIVE DEFICIT SPENDING** DURING WORLD WAR II HELPED END THE GREAT DEPRESSION.

IN SHORT, THE ECONOMISTS OF TODAY **DO NOT GIVE HIGH MARKS** TO THE ECONOMISTS OF THE 1930s.

YOU MISTAKENLY AMPUTATED **BOTH** MY LEGS?!

Heart Surgery Ward

AND EVEN WHEN THE ECONOMISTS OF THE 1930s **GOT THINGS RIGHT**...

...ELECTED OFFICIALS **MESSED THINGS UP ANYWAY.**

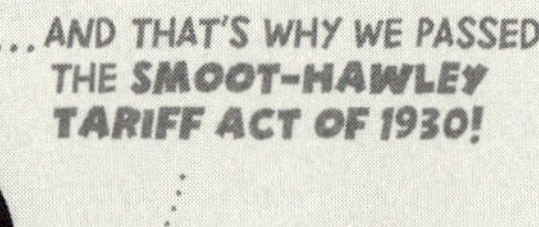

THE RESULT WAS THAT **EVERYBODY LOST.**

WE'VE LEARNED A LOT SINCE THE GREAT DEPRESSION, BUT THERE'S **ONE AREA** WHERE **WE STILL HAVE A LOT MORE TO LEARN.**

JUST LIKE **THE HEART** HELPS **CIRCULATE BLOOD** IN YOUR BODY...

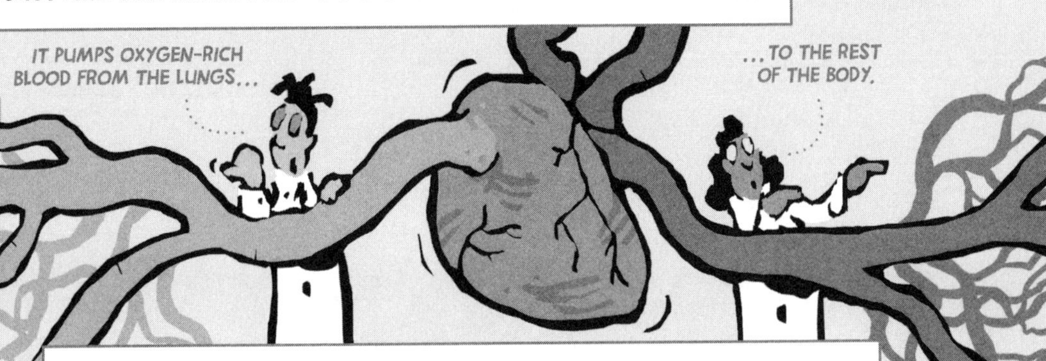

...BANKS AND OTHER FIRMS IN THE FINANCIAL SYSTEM HELP **CIRCULATE MONEY AND CREDIT** THROUGHOUT AN ECONOMY.

SO IT'S NO SURPRISE THAT **FAILURES IN THE FINANCIAL SYSTEM** CAN **SICKEN THE ENTIRE ECONOMY.**

UNFORTUNATELY, THESE FAILURES ARE **ALL TOO COMMON.**

THE TROUBLE WITH THE FINANCIAL SYSTEM IS THAT IT'S TRAPPED BETWEEN **MARKET FAILURE...**

...AND **GOVERNMENT FAILURE.**

ONE PROBLEM WITH THE FREE-MARKET APPROACH IS THAT BANKS BORROW MONEY **SHORT-TERM**...

...BUT LOAN IT OUT **LONG-TERM.**

THAT MAKES THEM VULNERABLE TO **BANK RUNS.**

BANK RUNS CAN DESTROY BANKS **EVEN IF THEY'RE HEALTHY...**

...AND LEAVE MANY DEPOSITORS WITH **NOTHING.**

IN ORDER TO AVOID BANK RUNS, MANY GOVERNMENTS OFFER **DEPOSIT INSURANCE**...

...BUT DEPOSIT INSURANCE FUNCTIONS AS A KIND OF **BAILOUT** THAT CAN PROMOTE **RISKY BEHAVIOR.**

SIMILAR CHALLENGES APPEAR THROUGHOUT THE FINANCIAL SYSTEM...

...GIVING RISE TO WHAT ECONOMISTS CALL **MORAL HAZARD.**

IN SUM, THE FINANCIAL SYSTEM IS A CRUCIAL PART OF THE ECONOMY THAT APPEARS TO BE **PRONE TO INSTABILITY.**

ECONOMISTS CONTINUE TO STRUGGLE TO CONTROL THE FINANCIAL SYSTEM...

...BUT IRONING OUT ALL THE KINKS MAY BE **IMPOSSIBLE.**

SO EVEN THOUGH MONETARY POLICY AND FISCAL POLICY HAVE **IMPROVED TREMENDOUSLY** SINCE THE GREAT DEPRESSION...

...WE'RE STILL A LONG WAY FROM SEEING **THE END** OF THE BUSINESS CYCLE.

CHAPTER 13
THE END OF POVERTY?

OF THE 7 BILLION OR SO PEOPLE ON EARTH IN 2010, ABOUT **1 BILLION** LIVE IN **RICH COUNTRIES**...

IN THE U.S., JAPAN, AND WESTERN EUROPE, PER CAPITA GDP IS OVER **$30,000 A YEAR.**

...ABOUT **4.5 BILLION** LIVE IN **MIDDLE-INCOME COUNTRIES**...

IN CHINA, BRAZIL, AND SOUTH AFRICA, PER CAPITA GDP IS THE EQUIVALENT OF ABOUT **$10,000 A YEAR.**

...AND ABOUT **1.5 BILLION** LIVE IN **LOW-INCOME COUNTRIES.**

IN PAKISTAN, NIGERIA, AND NICARAGUA, PER CAPITA GDP AVERAGES LESS THAN **$3,650 A YEAR**...

...ONLY A FEW DOLLARS A DAY.

IN LOW- AND MIDDLE-INCOME COUNTRIES, POVERTY IS SO WIDESPREAD THAT THE IDEA OF **ENDING POVERTY** SEEMS LIKE A **FANTASY.**

BUT ECONOMISTS HAVE A **WILDLY OPTIMISTIC** IDEA CALLED **CATCH-UP.**
WHAT'S CATCH-UP?
THE IDEA IS THAT **PER CAPITA GDP** IN **POORER COUNTRIES**...
...WILL **CONVERGE** WITH PER CAPITA GDP **IN RICHER COUNTRIES**...
...SO THAT EVENTUALLY **ALL COUNTRIES WILL BE RICH!**
OF COURSE, CATCH-UP WILL **TAKE TIME.**
SMELLS GREAT. WHEN IS IT GOING TO BE READY?
EVENTUALLY.

THE **GOOD NEWS** IS THAT CATCH-UP IS **MORE THAN JUST A DREAM.**

THE ECONOMIC THEORY BEHIND CATCH-UP IS THAT **ADDITIONAL INVESTMENTS ARE MORE PRODUCTIVE IN POOR COUNTRIES** THAN IN RICH COUNTRIES.

AS A RESULT, POOR COUNTRIES WILL NATURALLY **ATTRACT MORE INVESTMENT...**

...PUTTING THEM ON THE **ROAD TO RICHES.**

THE **BAD NEWS** IS THAT CATCH-UP IS **NOT THE WHOLE STORY**...

...AND THAT'S WHY MOST ECONOMISTS NOW SUPPORT THE IDEA OF **CONDITIONAL CONVERGENCE**.

FOR EXAMPLE, SOME ECONOMISTS THINK THAT POOR COUNTRIES ARE STUCK IN A **POVERTY TRAP...**

...AND THAT ALL THEY NEED TO GET ON THE ROAD TO RICHES IS A **BIG BOOST** TO BREAK THE CYCLE.

OTHER ECONOMISTS ARGUE THAT A POVERTY TRAP **ISN'T THE FUNDAMENTAL PROBLEM...**

...AND THAT THE RECIPE FOR GROWTH DEPENDS MORE ON **GOOD GOVERNMENT...**

...AND EVEN ON FACTORS LIKE **GEOGRAPHY.**

DEVELOPMENT ECONOMISTS MAY NOT AGREE ABOUT **EVERYTHING**...
THERE ARE **TOO MANY COOKS** IN THIS KITCHEN!

...BUT THEY DO AGREE ON **THE BASICS.**
IT'S BASICALLY **BEANS** AND **RICE** AND A LITTLE **SALT.**
YUP.
THAT'S TRUE.

COUNTRIES LIKE **CHINA** AND **INDIA** HAVE IMPLEMENTED SOME OF THESE **BASIC IDEAS...**
WE NOW HAVE A LARGELY **MARKET-BASED ECONOMY...**
...**PEACE AND STABILITY...**
...AND **OPENNESS TO WORLD TRADE!**

...AND ARE MAKING PROGRESS IN THE **LONG CLIMB OUT OF POVERTY.**
GOOD THING THIS LADDER HAS ROOM FOR **4 BILLION MORE PEOPLE!**

THESE SUCCESS STORIES MAKE ECONOMISTS **OPTIMISTIC** ABOUT DEFEATING GLOBAL POVERTY...

...BUT THEY'RE ALSO AWARE OF **TROUBLE SPOTS**.

THESE TROUBLE SPOTS POSE A DAUNTING CHALLENGE, ESPECIALLY IN **AFRICA**...

...AND THE FATE OF THE SO-CALLED **BOTTOM BILLION** IS A KEY QUESTION FOR THE 21ST CENTURY.

OVERALL, HOWEVER, THE VISION OF POOR COUNTRIES **CATCHING UP** WITH RICH COUNTRIES IS **COMPELLING**...

I CAN SEE THE MOUNTAINTOP!

IT'S THE **END OF POVERTY.**

WE'RE ALMOST THERE!

...SO COMPELLING THAT IT'S EASY TO **LOSE SIGHT OF REALITY.**

THERE'S **POVERTY IN RICH COUNTRIES TOO.**

OOPS.

SIMPLY **DEFINING POVERTY** CAN BE DIFFICULT IN THE RICH WORLD...

...AND SOME ECONOMISTS ARGUE THAT THE FOCUS SHOULD BE ON **RELATIVE POVERTY.**

HOWEVER YOU DEFINE IT, **THE WAY TO REDUCE POVERTY** IN RICH COUNTRIES IS CLEAR...

...BUT GETTING INTO THE DETAILS WOULD REQUIRE A **WHOLE DIFFERENT BOOK.**

SADLY, POVERTY IS **NOT GOING TO END** IN THE 21ST CENTURY.

BUT THE GLOBAL LANDSCAPE IS **RAPIDLY SHIFTING**...

...AWAY FROM ISLANDS OF AFFLUENCE AMID A **SEA OF SCARCITY**...

...AND TOWARD A **RICHER AND MORE PROSPEROUS WORLD.**

CHAPTER 14
THE END OF PLANET EARTH?

BY 2050 THE NUMBER OF PEOPLE ON PLANET EARTH IS PROJECTED TO HIT 9 BILLION...
HAPPY BIRTHDAY TO YOU!
AND TO THE 24 MILLION OTHER PEOPLE WHO SHARE YOUR BIRTHDAY!
...UP FROM JUST 1 BILLION IN THE YEAR 1800 AND ONLY 6 BILLION IN THE YEAR 2000.
COMING SOON: 50% More Humans!
AND, AS WE SAW IN THE LAST CHAPTER, MANY OF THESE PEOPLE ARE LIKELY TO BE MUCH RICHER THAN THEIR PARENTS AND GRANDPARENTS.
GOODBYE, POVERTY...
...HELLO, WASHING MACHINE, REFRIGERATOR, AND AIR CONDITIONER!

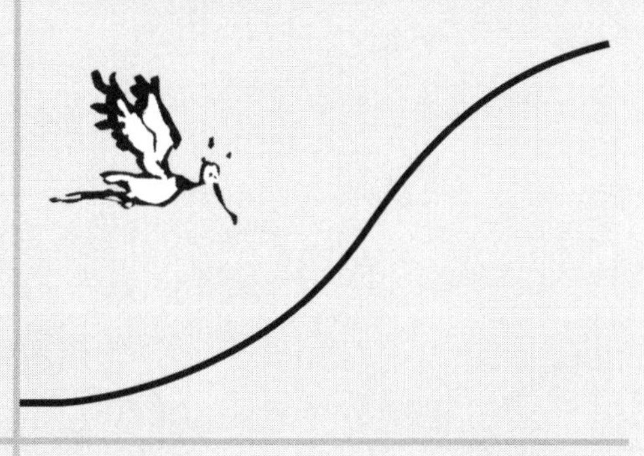

...RAISES CONCERNS ABOUT **RUNNING OUT** OF FOOD, MINERALS, AND OTHER VALUABLE NATURAL RESOURCES...

...AND ABOUT PROBLEMS LIKE **GLOBAL WARMING.**

EXPERT OPINION ABOUT THE **FATE OF THE PLANET** RANGES FROM **PESSIMISM**...

I WOULDN'T BE SHOCKED IF BY 2100 **MOST THINGS HAVE BEEN DESTROYED.**

NOTHING COULD BE MORE **MISLEADING** TO OUR CHILDREN THAN OUR PRESENT **AFFLUENT SOCIETY.**

WE CAN'T KEEP **THROWING EVERYTHING IN THE GARBAGE.**

WE HAVE TO **RECYCLE.**

THE END IS NEAR!

...TO **OPTIMISM.**

THE **BEST** IS **YET TO COME!**

WITHIN A CENTURY OR TWO...

...MOST OF HUMANITY WILL BE **AT OR ABOVE** TODAY'S WESTERN LIVING STANDARDS.

RECYCLING **IS** GARBAGE!

THE END OF POVERTY IS NEAR!

THE **PESSIMISTS** ARE WORRIED THAT HUMAN CIVILIZATION IS HEADING **TOWARD THE EDGE OF A CLIFF.**

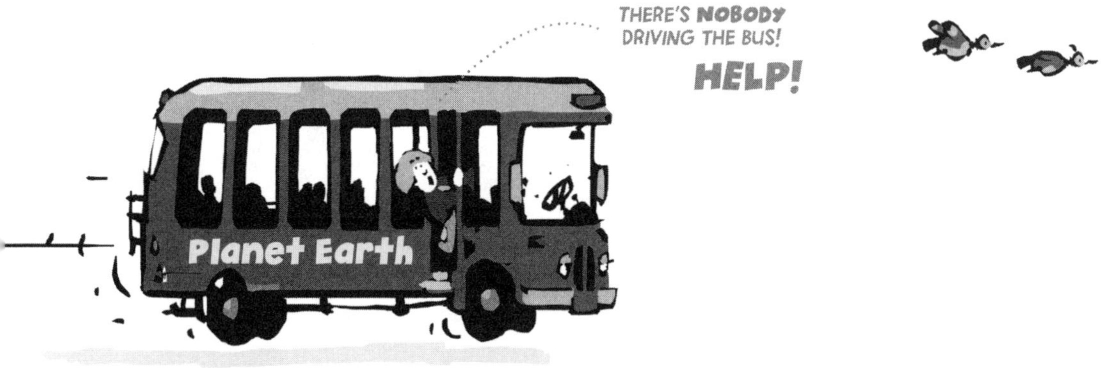

THE **OPTIMISTS** ARE CONVINCED THAT EVERYTHING WILL BE **FINE**...

...IN LARGE PART BECAUSE OF THEIR FAITH IN **FREE-MARKET ECONOMICS.**

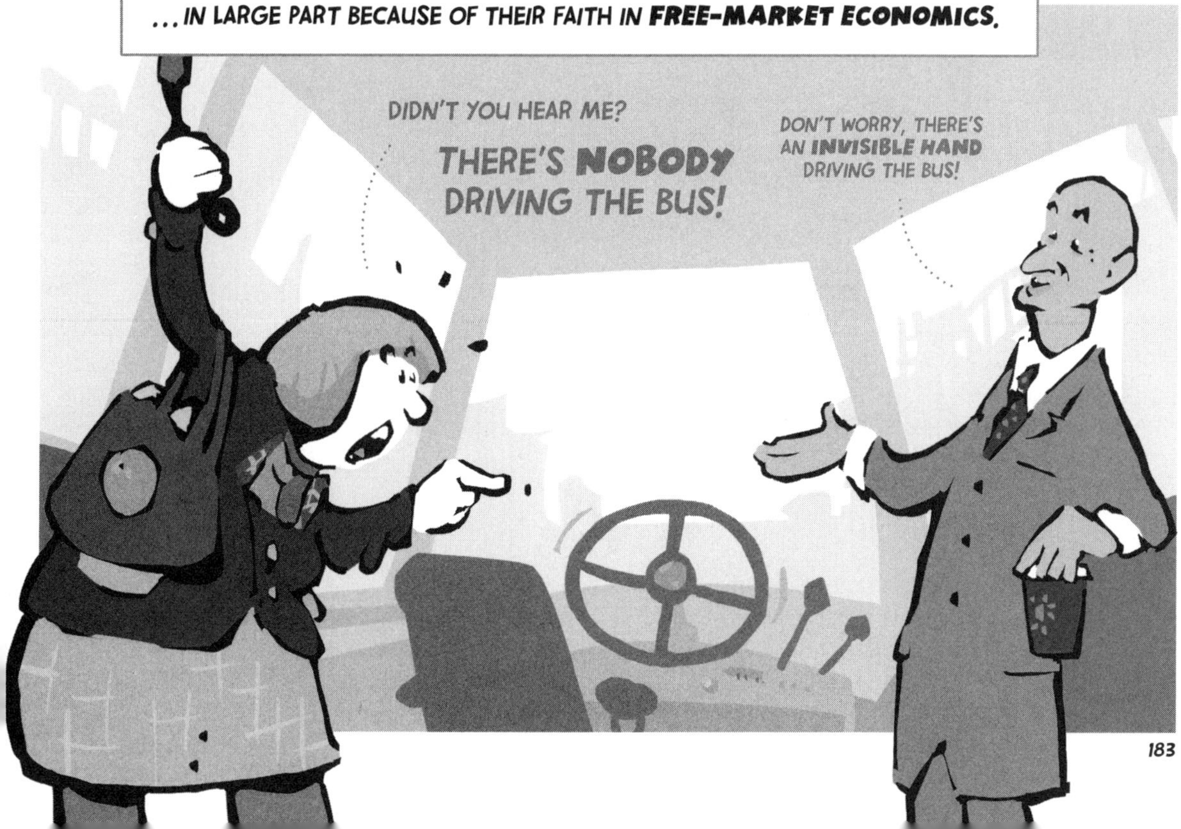

DIDN'T YOU HEAR ME?

THERE'S **NOBODY** DRIVING THE BUS!

DON'T WORRY, THERE'S AN **INVISIBLE HAND** DRIVING THE BUS!

ECONOMISTS HAVE A LOT TO SAY ABOUT THE DEBATE BETWEEN THE OPTIMISTS AND THE PESSIMISTS.

THE BASIC PESSIMIST ARGUMENT GOES BACK TO THE 18TH-CENTURY PHILOSOPHER **THOMAS MALTHUS**.

FORTUNATELY, MALTHUS **WAS WRONG**...

...AND MODERN-DAY PESSIMISTS HAVE A **LONG HISTORY OF SIMILAR FAILURES**.

WHAT THE PESSIMISTS DON'T SEE IS THAT **FREE MARKETS OFTEN WORK MIRACLES.**

FOR EXAMPLE, MARKETS FOR COPPER AND MANY OTHER **NATURAL RESOURCES** ARE WELL EQUIPPED TO DEAL WITH THE POSSIBILITY OF **INCREASING SCARCITY.**

IF **COPPER** BECOMES SCARCE, THEN THE **PRICE OF COPPER** WILL GO UP...

...AND THAT WILL PROVIDE INCENTIVES FOR PEOPLE TO **FIND NEW SOURCES...**

...AND TO **CONSERVE** THE COPPER WE HAVE NOW...

...AND TO **DISCOVER ALTERNATIVES.**

IN SHORT, WHEN MARKETS ARE WORKING WELL, ECONOMISTS ARE HAPPY PUTTING THE **INVISIBLE HAND** IN CHARGE OF THE FUTURE.

BUT WELL-FUNCTIONING MARKETS ARE **NOT THE END OF THE STORY.**

WHAT THE OPTIMISTS FAIL TO SEE IS THAT MARKETS **DON'T ALWAYS WORK WELL...**

...AND THAT HAS MADE THE OPTIMISTS BLIND TO **MARKET FAILURES LIKE CLIMATE CHANGE.**

WE SAW LOTS OF EXAMPLES OF **MARKET FAILURE** IN THE **MICRO** BOOK . . .

. . . AND SOMETIMES THE RESULTS ARE SO BAD THAT THEY'RE VISIBLE AT THE **MACRO** LEVEL.

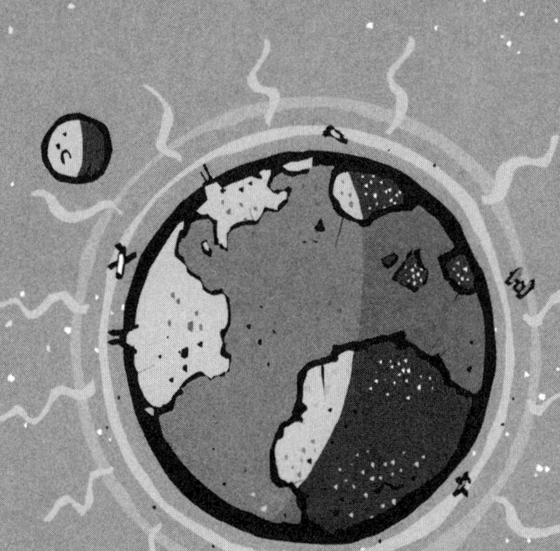

HERE'S WHAT **ECONOMISTS** NEED TO KNOW ABOUT **CLIMATE SCIENCE:**

FIRST, WE'RE ADDING **BILLIONS OF TONS OF CO_2** TO THE ATMOSPHERE **EACH YEAR.**

SECOND, **100 YEARS OF SCIENTIFIC THEORY** PREDICTS THAT THIS WILL **INCREASE GLOBAL AVERAGE TEMPERATURES** AND OTHERWISE CHANGE THE CLIMATE.

THIRD, WE'VE BEEN TESTING THIS THEORY IN A **PLANETARY EXPERIMENT**...

LET'S SEE WHAT HAPPENS IF WE **DOUBLE** THE AMOUNT OF CO_2 IN THE ATMOSPHERE!

UM, COULDN'T WE DO THIS TEST ON A **DIFFERENT PLANET?**

SORRY, THIS IS THE **ONLY ONE THAT'S AVAILABLE.**

...AND THE EVIDENCE SO FAR **SUPPORTS THE THEORY.**

WE PREDICTED THAT AVERAGE TEMPERATURES WOULD RISE ABOUT **0.36 DEGREES FAHRENHEIT EACH DECADE**...

...AND THOSE PREDICTIONS HAVE BEEN PRETTY CLOSE TO THE MARK!

THAT'S WHY ALMOST ALL **SCIENTISTS AGREE** THAT **MOST** OF THE INCREASE IN GLOBAL AVERAGE TEMPERATURE SINCE THE MID-20TH CENTURY...

...IS VERY LIKELY DUE TO **HUMAN ACTIVITY.**

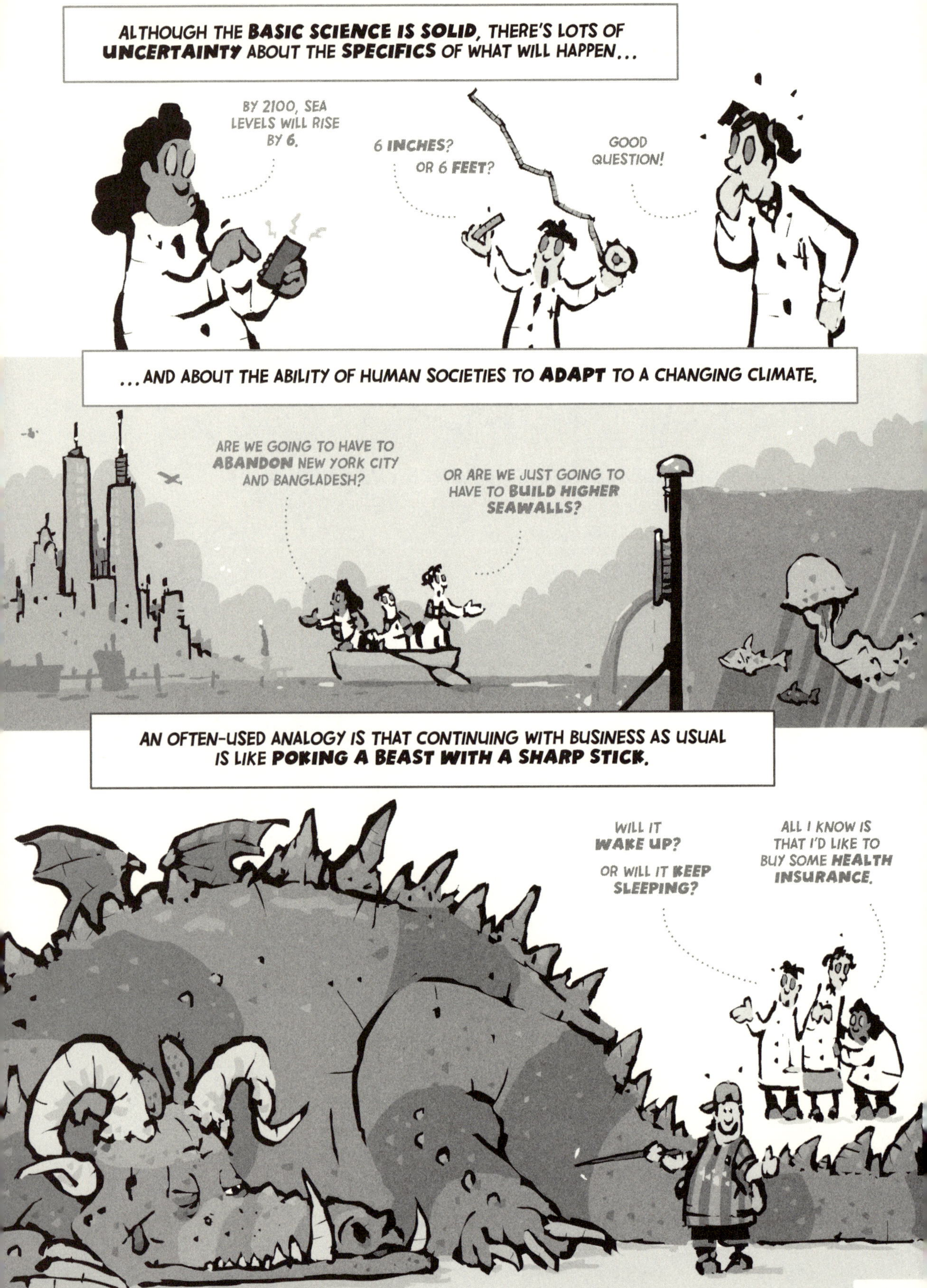

ALTHOUGH THE **BASIC SCIENCE IS SOLID**, THERE'S LOTS OF **UNCERTAINTY** ABOUT THE **SPECIFICS** OF WHAT WILL HAPPEN...

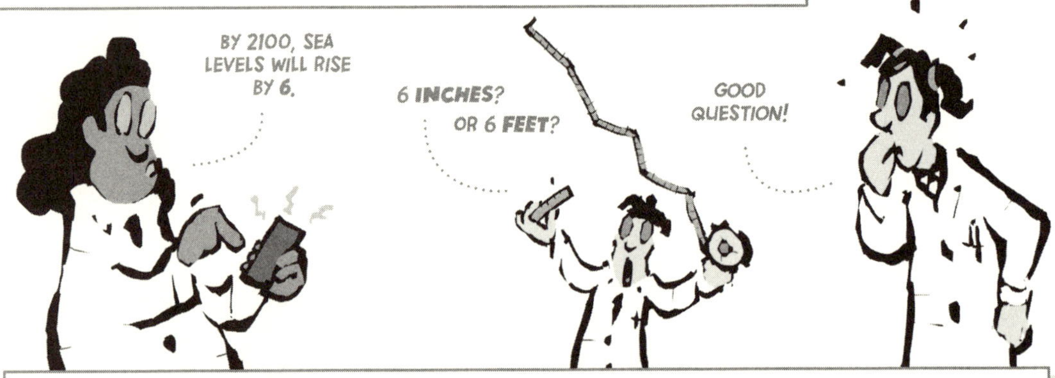

...AND ABOUT THE ABILITY OF HUMAN SOCIETIES TO **ADAPT** TO A CHANGING CLIMATE.

AN OFTEN-USED ANALOGY IS THAT CONTINUING WITH BUSINESS AS USUAL IS LIKE **POKING A BEAST WITH A SHARP STICK**.

WILL IT **WAKE UP?** OR WILL IT **KEEP SLEEPING?**

ALL I KNOW IS THAT I'D LIKE TO BUY SOME **HEALTH INSURANCE**.

THESE UNCERTAINTIES ARE A BIG REASON ECONOMISTS **DON'T AGREE** ABOUT **HOW AGGRESSIVELY** WE SHOULD FIGHT CLIMATE CHANGE...

...BUT THEY **DO AGREE** THAT THE **BEST WAY** TO FIGHT CLIMATE CHANGE IS WITH THE **TOOLS OF ECONOMICS.**

MARKET FORCES ARE THE MOST POWERFUL WAY TO PROMOTE INNOVATION IN **CLEAN TECHNOLOGY**...

...AND THE BEST WAY TO HARNESS **MARKET FORCES** IS TO **PUT A PRICE ON CARBON.**

THE BIG PICTURE IS THAT ECONOMISTS DON'T WORRY THAT WE'LL RUN OUT OF NATURAL RESOURCES LIKE COPPER...
WHEN YOU HAVE WELL-FUNCTIONING MARKETS...
...YOU CAN ENTRUST THE FUTURE TO THE INVISIBLE HAND.
...BUT THEY DO WORRY ABOUT PROBLEMS LIKE CLIMATE CHANGE...
IT'S THE GREATEST MARKET FAILURE THE WORLD HAS EVER SEEN.
CARBON PRICING NOW!
...AND THIS GIVES ECONOMISTS A UNIQUE PERSPECTIVE ON THE ENVIRONMENTAL CHALLENGES OF THE 21ST CENTURY.
WE'RE NOT WORRIED ABOUT RUNNING OUT OF FOSSIL FUELS...
...WE'RE WORRIED ABOUT NOT RUNNING OUT OF FOSSIL FUELS!

CHAPTER 15

THE END OF YOUTH?

IN THE 20TH CENTURY, MACROECONOMIES WERE LIKE **YOUNG FAMILIES**...

...BUT IN THE 21ST CENTURY, THEY'RE **SHOWING SOME SIGNS OF AGE.**

AGING POPULATIONS ARE MOST NOTICEABLE IN **RICH COUNTRIES**...

...WHERE THE TREND IS BEING ACCENTUATED BY THE **RETIREMENT OF THE BABY BOOMERS.**

BUT **POOR COUNTRIES** ARE ALSO STARTING TO GO THROUGH THE DEMOGRAPHIC TRANSITION FROM **YOUTH** TO **MATURITY.**

BUT INCREASING LIFE SPANS WILL REQUIRE ADJUSTMENTS FROM **INDIVIDUALS**...

...FROM **FAMILIES**...

...AND FROM **GOVERNMENTS.**

IN THE U.S., AGING IS LIKELY TO BE **ESPECIALLY DIFFICULT**...

...FOR **SOCIAL SECURITY**...

...AND **MEDICARE.**

THESE FEDERAL GOVERNMENT PROGRAMS ARE **SO BIG**, THEY MAKE UP A SIGNIFICANT PORTION OF THE **ENTIRE U.S. GDP.**

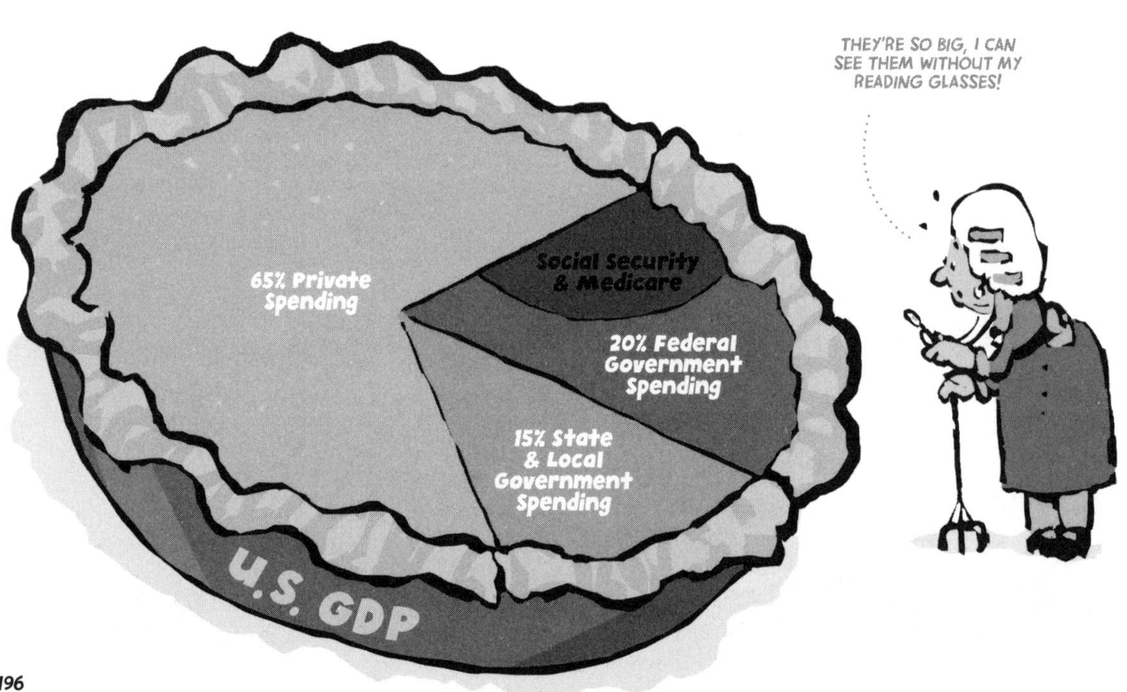

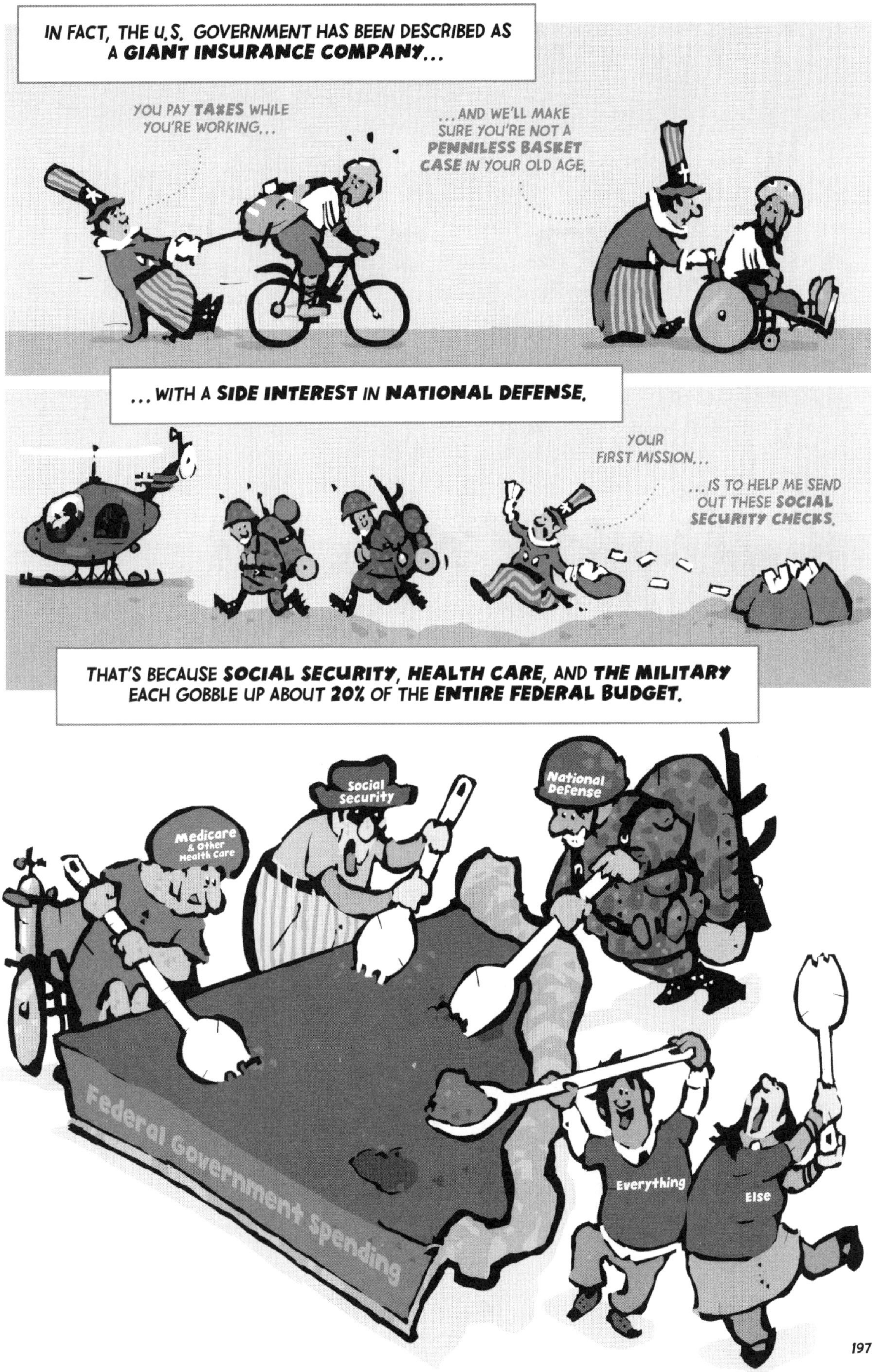

IN FACT, THE U.S. GOVERNMENT HAS BEEN DESCRIBED AS A **GIANT INSURANCE COMPANY**...

...WITH A **SIDE INTEREST** IN **NATIONAL DEFENSE.**

THAT'S BECAUSE **SOCIAL SECURITY**, **HEALTH CARE**, AND **THE MILITARY** EACH GOBBLE UP ABOUT **20%** OF THE **ENTIRE FEDERAL BUDGET.**

WHILE IT'S TEMPTING TO COMPARE MEDICARE AND SOCIAL SECURITY TO **INDIVIDUAL RETIREMENT ACCOUNTS**...

...THEY ACTUALLY WORK MORE LIKE A **BUCKET BRIGADE.**

FORMALLY, THIS BUCKET BRIGADE SYSTEM IS KNOWN BY A NIFTY ACRONYM:

PAYGO.

INFORMALLY, IT'S KNOWN AS **TROUBLE.**

TAXES PAID BY WORKERS ARE ENOUGH TO COVER THE PROMISES MADE TO RETIREES **RIGHT NOW.**

BETWEEN 2010 AND 2050, HOWEVER, THE PORTION OF GDP GOBBLED UP BY SOCIAL SECURITY IS PROJECTED TO **INCREASE BY 25%...**

...AND THE PORTION CONSUMED BY MEDICARE IS PROJECTED TO ALMOST **DOUBLE.**

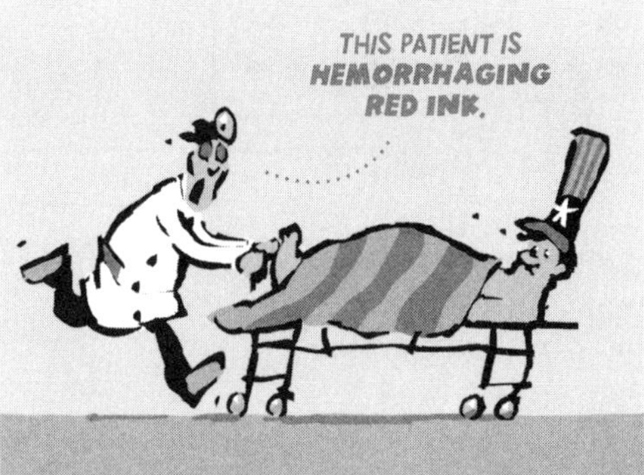

SINCE THE PORTION OF GDP CONTRIBUTED BY WORKERS IS LIKELY TO **STAY ABOUT THE SAME...**

...THAT MEANS THE BUCKET BRIGADE IS **HEADED FOR A BREAKDOWN.**

DEALING WITH SOCIAL SECURITY AND MEDICARE IS LIKELY TO INVOLVE SOME COMBINATION OF **THREE PAINFUL OPTIONS.**
PICK YOUR POISON.
THE GOVERNMENT CAN **CUT BENEFITS...**
WHAT? NO WAY!
...**INCREASE TAXES...**
WHAT? NO WAY!
...OR **BORROW THE MONEY.**
WAAAHHH!

TWO OTHER **POTENTIAL SOLUTIONS** ARE **RELATIVELY PAINLESS...**

PAINLESS?

THAT SOUNDS **GOOD!**

GOO!

...BUT THEY BOTH FACE **BIG CHALLENGES.**

ONE IDEA IS TO **IMPROVE EFFICIENCY** BY FINDING **CHEAPER WAYS** TO PROVIDE HEALTH CARE.

THE **OTHER** RELATIVELY PAINLESS SOLUTION IS TO SIMPLY **GROW OUR WAY OUT** OF OUR FINANCIAL PROBLEMS...

...JUST LIKE A FAMILY WITH **GROWING INCOME** CAN MORE EASILY SUPPORT AGING PARENTS.

BUT THIS RUNS INTO **ANOTHER DIFFICULTY**: IT'S NOT JUST **PEOPLE** THAT ARE SLOWING DOWN.

THE **RATE OF TECHNOLOGICAL PROGRESS** MIGHT BE **SLOWING DOWN TOO.**

THE IDEA THAT TECHNOLOGICAL PROGRESS IS SLOWING DOWN MIGHT SEEM ABSURD...
Newer!
Faster!
Smaller!
...BUT IT BECOMES MORE PLAUSIBLE WHEN YOU TAKE A CLOSER LOOK AT HISTORY.

WHAT HAVE YOU GOT THAT'S AS REVOLUTIONARY AS THE TELEGRAPH?
ER...

OR THE STEAM ENGINE?
UM...

OR THE WHEEL?

ECONOMISTS MEASURE THE **ECONOMIC IMPACT** OF NEW TECHNOLOGIES BY LOOKING AT HOW THEY AFFECT **WORKER PRODUCTIVITY**...

...AND THE FACT IS THAT AFTER A **GOLDEN AGE IN THE MID-20TH CENTURY**...

WE'VE GOT ELECTRICITY!

AND THE INTERNAL COMBUSTION ENGINE!

...THE GROWTH IN WORKER PRODUCTIVITY **SLOWED DOWN**.

OF COURSE, THERE'S ALWAYS HOPE THAT **PRODUCTIVITY GROWTH WILL PICK UP AGAIN**...

...BUT FOR NOW ECONOMISTS ARE STILL WRESTLING WITH AN OBSERVATION NOBEL PRIZE WINNER **ROBERT SOLOW** MADE IN 1987 ABOUT **ECONOMIC GROWTH**.

FOR BETTER OR WORSE, THE U.S. IS NOT ALONE IN DEALING WITH BOTH DEMOGRAPHIC AND TECHNOLOGICAL AGING.
MISERY LOVES COMPANY!
MOST COUNTRIES IN THE RICH WORLD ARE HEADING TOWARD SERIOUS DEBT PROBLEMS.
TRYING TO FIX OUR BUDGET PROBLEMS...
...IS AS HARD AS TRYING TO GET GRANDPA TO STOP DRIVING!
AND WHILE MOST POOR COUNTRIES ARE AVOIDING DEBT PROBLEMS...
...IT'S ONLY BECAUSE THEIR SOCIAL SAFETY NETS ARE PRETTY WEAK.
OUR GOVERNMENT FINANCES ARE AGING NICELY...
...BUT OUR SENIOR CITIZENS ARE NOT.

AS WE HEAD INTO THE 21ST CENTURY, ALMOST ALL COUNTRIES WILL FACE A DIFFICULT CONFLICT BETWEEN WHAT SEEMS TO BE **MORALLY RIGHT**...

...AND WHAT SEEMS TO BE **ECONOMICALLY SUSTAINABLE**.

CHAPTER 16
THE END

...THIS **MACROECONOMICS** BOOK **STARTED SMALL**...

macro

WE'RE A SINGLE ECONOMY.

...AND THEN GOT **BIGGER**...

INTERNATIONAL TRADE!

...AND **BIGGER.**

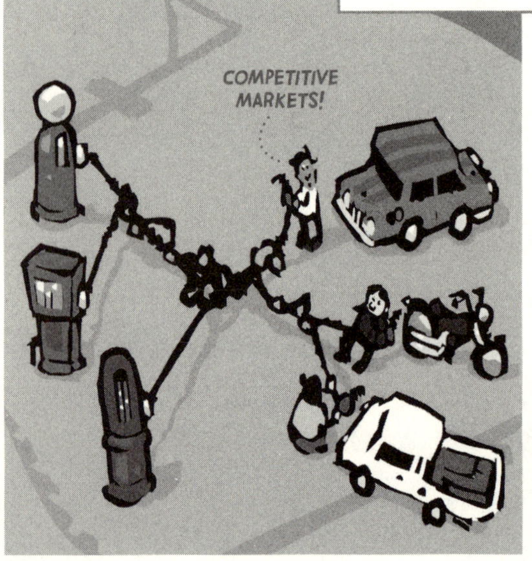

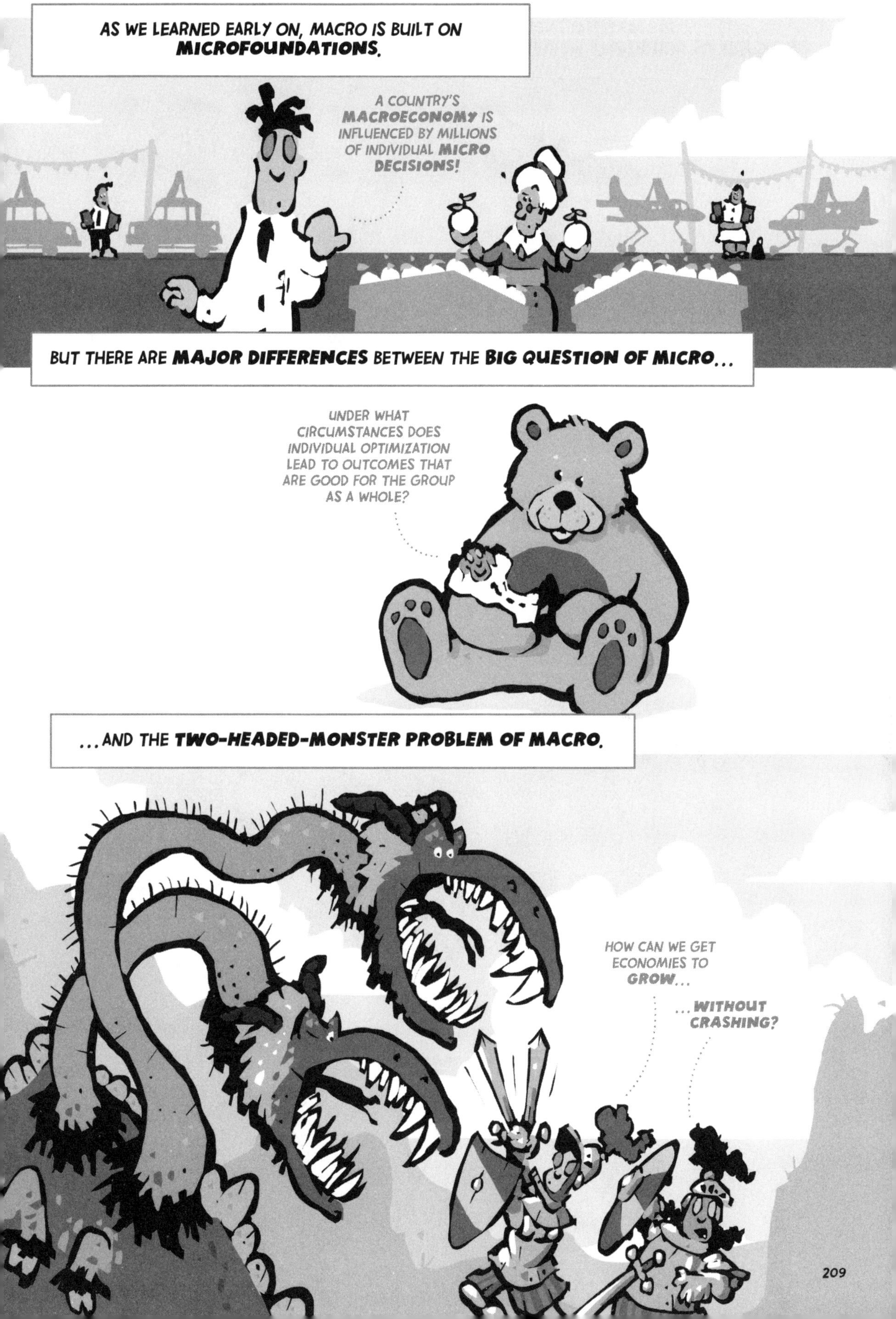

AS WE LEARNED EARLY ON, MACRO IS BUILT ON **MICROFOUNDATIONS.**

BUT THERE ARE **MAJOR DIFFERENCES** BETWEEN THE **BIG QUESTION OF MICRO...**

...AND THE **TWO-HEADED-MONSTER PROBLEM OF MACRO.**

HOW CAN WE GET ECONOMIES TO **GROW...**

...**WITHOUT CRASHING?**

ONE BIG DIFFERENCE BETWEEN MICRO AND MACRO IS THAT **MACRO IS HAVING MORE TROUBLE TAMING ITS MONSTERS.**

BECAUSE OF THESE STRUGGLES, A **MACRO BOOK** IN **2100** COULD LOOK **RADICALLY DIFFERENT** THAN THIS ONE...

... JUST AS **TODAY'S MACRO** LOOKS RADICALLY DIFFERENT THAN IT DID IN 1900.

IN CONTRAST, A **MICRO BOOK** IN **2100** WILL ALMOST CERTAINLY LOOK JUST ABOUT THE **SAME AS IT DOES TODAY.**

FUNDAMENTALLY, MICRO IS STABLE BECAUSE IT FOCUSES ON ONE BASIC STORY...
ONCE UPON A TIME THERE WAS AN OPTIMIZING INDIVIDUAL...
...THE REST IS JUST MATH!
...AND MACRO IS UNSTABLE BECAUSE IT HAS COMPETING STORIES ABOUT THE NATURE OF THE ECONOMY...
THE ECONOMY IS LIKE A WELL-ORGANIZED FAMILY!
NO, IT'S LIKE A DYSFUNCTIONAL FAMILY!
...AND THE ROLE OF GOVERNMENT.
THE GOVERNMENT IS A GOOD PARENT THAT CAN PROMOTE GROWTH AND STABILITY!
NO, IT'S A BAD PARENT THAT SHOULD BE INVOLVED AS LITTLE AS POSSIBLE!

...AS WITH THE **NEOCLASSICAL SYNTHESIS**...

...OR THE **WASHINGTON CONSENSUS.**

THE WAY TO HELP **POOR COUNTRIES BECOME RICH**...

...IS TO **PROMOTE INTERNATIONAL TRADE**...

...**BALANCED GOVERNMENT BUDGETS**...

...AND **FREE MARKETS.**

AT OTHER TIMES IT SEEMS AS IF MACROECONOMISTS ARE **HOPELESSLY FAR APART.**

ALTHOUGH THE DISAGREEMENTS BETWEEN MACROECONOMISTS ARE **EASY TO JOKE ABOUT**...

DEBATES ABOUT **MERCANTILISM**...

...OR **SELF-SUFFICIENCY**...

ECONOMIC GROWTH COMES FROM **DOING EVERYTHING OURSELVES!**

...SEEM POSITIVELY **OLD-FASHIONED** NOW THAT MACROECONOMISTS HAVE A **BETTER UNDERSTANDING OF INTERNATIONAL TRADE.**

TRADE CREATES **LOSERS** AS WELL AS **WINNERS**...

...BUT IN THE LONG RUN IT'S **PRETTY AWESOME** FOR **EVERYBODY.**

JUST LIKE TECHNOLOGICAL PROGRESS!

SIMILARLY, GIVEN WHAT WE NOW KNOW ABOUT **MONETARY POLICY**...

...IT'S AMAZING TO LOOK BACK AT FIGHTS ABOUT THINGS LIKE THE **GOLD STANDARD.**

AND MACROECONOMISTS HAVE LEARNED A GREAT DEAL FROM THE **MISTAKES OF THE GREAT DEPRESSION.**

...BY WHAT ALAN BLINDER CALLS AN ECONOMICS VERSION OF **MURPHY'S LAW.**

THE PROBLEM IS THAT THE GENERAL PUBLIC DOESN'T SEEM TO PAY MUCH ATTENTION WHEN ECONOMISTS **AGREE WITH ONE ANOTHER**...

...BUT PEOPLE CAN'T SEEM TO GET ENOUGH OF **WATCHING ECONOMISTS FIGHT.**

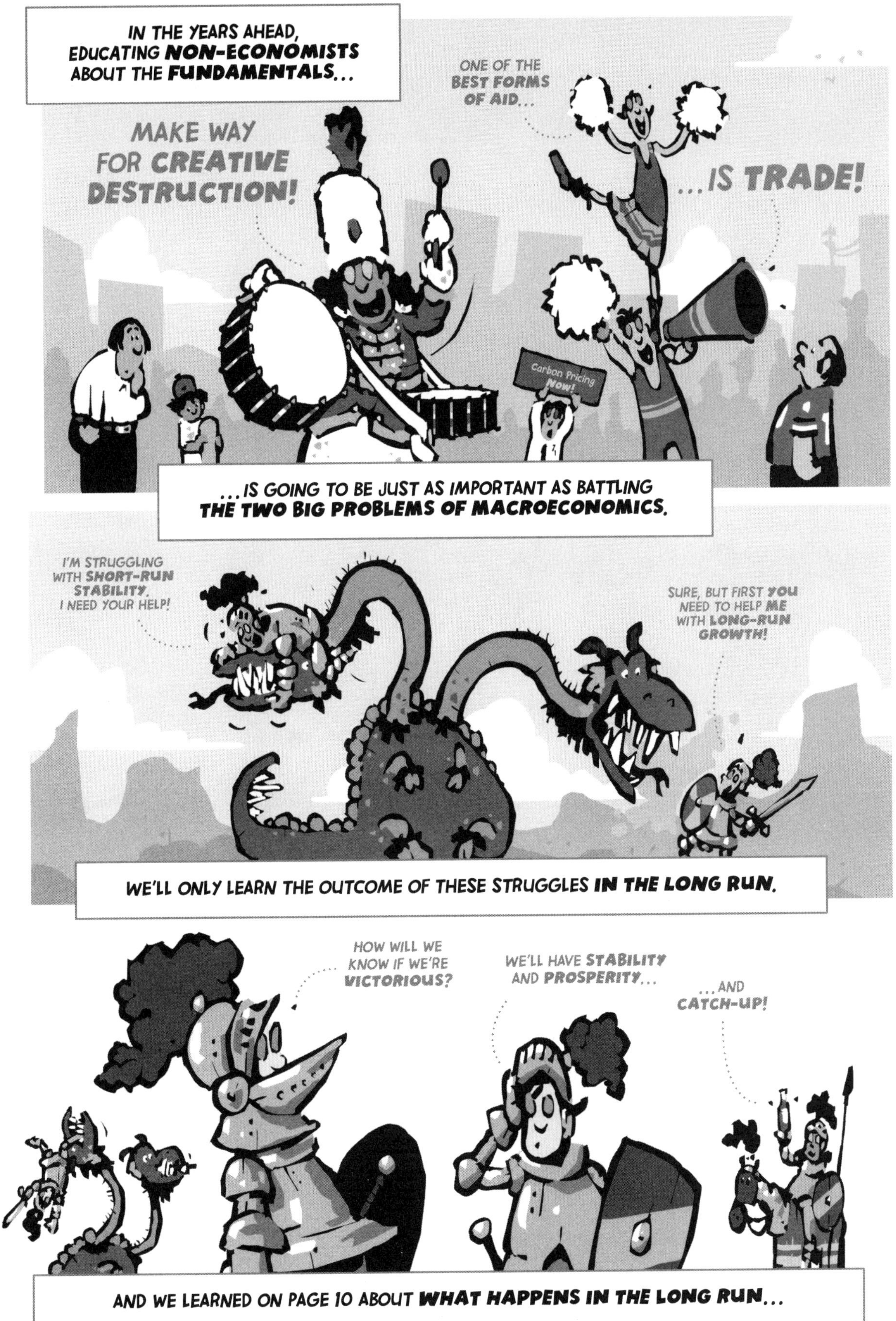

IN THE YEARS AHEAD, EDUCATING **NON-ECONOMISTS** ABOUT THE **FUNDAMENTALS...**

MAKE WAY FOR **CREATIVE DESTRUCTION!**

ONE OF THE **BEST FORMS OF AID...**

...IS **TRADE!**

Carbon Pricing **Now!**

...IS GOING TO BE JUST AS IMPORTANT AS BATTLING **THE TWO BIG PROBLEMS OF MACROECONOMICS.**

I'M STRUGGLING WITH **SHORT-RUN STABILITY.** I NEED YOUR HELP!

SURE, BUT FIRST **YOU** NEED TO HELP **ME** WITH **LONG-RUN GROWTH!**

WE'LL ONLY LEARN THE OUTCOME OF THESE STRUGGLES **IN THE LONG RUN.**

AND WE LEARNED ON PAGE 10 ABOUT **WHAT HAPPENS IN THE LONG RUN...**

BURIED HERE
ARE THE BRAVE
ECONOMISTS...
...WHO FOUND
THE SECRET
TO SHORT-RUN
STABILITY
AND LONG-RUN
GROWTH.
OR DID THEY???

GLOSSARY

A

AUTOMATIC STABILIZERS
TAXES OR SPENDING PROGRAMS—SUCH AS UNEMPLOYMENT BENEFITS, WHICH RISE DURING RECESSIONS AND FALL DURING EXPANSIONS—THAT NATURALLY ACT TO COUNTER THE BUSINESS CYCLE: 77

B

BANK RUN
A PANIC IN WHICH DEPOSITORS ALL TRY TO WITHDRAW MONEY FROM A BANK AT THE SAME TIME: 164

BOND
IN RETURN FOR LENDING MONEY TO A COMPANY OR GOVERNMENT, THE LENDER GETS A BOND, WHICH OBLIGATES THE BORROWER TO PAY BACK THE LOAN (PLUS INTEREST) AFTER A SPECIFIED PERIOD OF TIME: 40–43

BUDGET DEFICIT / SURPLUS
A GOVERNMENT RUNS A **BUDGET DEFICIT** IN A GIVEN YEAR IF REVENUES (MONEY IN) ARE LESS THAN EXPENDITURES (MONEY OUT), A **BUDGET SURPLUS** IF REVENUES ARE GREATER THAN EXPENDITURES, AND A **BALANCED BUDGET** IF THE TWO ARE EQUAL; THE ACCUMULATION OF ALL ANNUAL **NATIONAL DEFICITS** IS THE **NATIONAL DEBT**: 79, 149, 160–161

BUSINESS CYCLE
SHORT-TERM ECONOMIC FLUCTUATIONS: 11, 113, 153–166
AND CYCLICAL UNEMPLOYMENT: 26

C

CARBON PRICING
A CARBON TAX OR CAP-AND-TRADE POLICY THAT SEEKS TO REDUCE CARBON EMISSIONS BY MAKING POLLUTING EXPENSIVE: 191–192, 217

COMPARATIVE ADVANTAGE
THE IDEA THAT TWO INDIVIDUALS (OR TWO COUNTRIES) CAN BOTH GAIN FROM TRADE EVEN IF ONE OF THEM IS BETTER THAN THE OTHER AT EVERYTHING: 101, 136

CAPITAL
MACHINERY, HOUSES, OR OTHER ASSETS: 91
CAPITAL INCOME: 62

CATCH-UP

THE IDEA—ALSO CALLED **CONVERGENCE**—THAT POOR COUNTRIES WILL GROW FASTER THAN RICH COUNTRIES: **169–171**

CENTRAL BANK

A GOVERNMENT AGENCY (SUCH AS THE EUROPEAN CENTRAL BANK OR THE FED) THAT IS IN CHARGE OF THE MONEY SUPPLY: **37**

CLASSICAL ECONOMICS

A SCHOOL OF THOUGHT THAT VIEWS THE ECONOMY AS A WELL-ORGANIZED FAMILY AND THEREFORE SEES LITTLE NEED FOR GOVERNMENT INTERVENTION: **9**

- CONTRAST WITH KEYNESIAN ECONOMICS: **12–13, 18–19, 22, 27**
- AND THE LABOR MARKET: **19–21**
- AND MONEY NEUTRALITY: **35**
- AND TRADE: **99–110**
- AND NEOCLASSICAL SYNTHESIS: **212**

CLIMATE CHANGE / GLOBAL WARMING

AN INCREASE IN GLOBAL AVERAGE TEMPERATURE, ESPECIALLY AS A RESULT OF BURNING FOSSIL FUELS AND OTHER HUMAN ACTIVITIES: **115, 181, 186–192**

CONDITIONAL AID

FOREIGN AID THAT IS PROVIDED WITH STRINGS ATTACHED: **133**

CONSUMER PRICE INDEX (CPI)

A WAY TO MEASURE INFLATION IN CONSUMER PRICES: **46–47, 51**

- COMPARED TO GDP DEFLATOR: **222**

THE CPI COMPARES PRICES IN YEARS X AND Y BY TRACKING THE COST OF A **REPRESENTATIVE BUNDLE** OF CONSUMER GOODS AND SERVICES. HERE'S AN EXAMPLE:

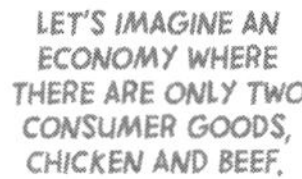

	PRICE OF CHICKEN	POUNDS OF CHICKEN IN BUNDLE	PRICE OF BEEF	POUNDS OF BEEF IN BUNDLE
YEAR X	$1/POUND	200	$3/POUND	100
YEAR Y	$2/POUND	200	$4/POUND	100

FIRST WE CALCULATE **THE BUNDLE'S PRICE IN YEAR X:**

(\$1 X 200) + (\$3 X 100) = **\$500.**

THEN WE CALCULATE **THE BUNDLE'S PRICE IN YEAR Y:**

(\$2 X 200) + (\$4 X 100) = **\$800.**

FINALLY, WE CONCLUDE THAT INFLATION (AS MEASURED BY THE CPI) WAS **60%** BETWEEN YEAR X AND YEAR Y BY COMPARING THE TWO:

$$\frac{\$800}{\$500} - 1 = 0.60$$

CREATIVE DESTRUCTION
ECONOMIC DEVELOPMENTS THAT BOTH CREATE AND DESTROY JOBS: **20–21, 109, 217**

CROWDING OUT
THE IDEA THAT GOVERNMENT ACTIVITY NEGATIVELY AFFECTS BUSINESS: FOR EXAMPLE, THAT BUDGET DEFICITS MAKE IT HARDER FOR BUSINESSES TO BORROW MONEY: **83**

CURRENCY
THE MONEY USED IN A COUNTRY: **139–150**
- CURRENCY MANIPULATION: **108–109**
- STRONG AND WEAK CURRENCIES: **142–143**

CURRENCY UNION
THE USE OF THE SAME CURRENCY IN MULTIPLE COUNTRIES: **146–150**

D

DEFICIT
SEE **BUDGET DEFICIT**

DEFLATION
A GENERAL DECREASE IN PRICES OVER TIME (THE OPPOSITE OF INFLATION): **55–56**

DEPRESSION
A VERY BAD RECESSION: **18, 154**

E

EFFICIENCY WAGES
THE THEORY THAT EMPLOYERS PAY HIGH WAGES IN ORDER TO AVOID TURNOVER AND MOTIVATE EMPLOYEES: **24**

EXCHANGE RATE
A WAY TO COMPARE THE VALUE OF DIFFERENT CURRENCIES: **140–150**

MARKET EXCHANGE RATES ARE EITHER **FLOATING** (IF THEY'RE BASED ON SUPPLY AND DEMAND) OR **FIXED** (IF THEY'RE PEGGED AT A SET RATE BY ONE OR MORE GOVERNMENTS). BECAUSE SOME GOODS ARE NOT TRADED INTERNATIONALLY, COMPARISONS OF LIVING STANDARDS IN DIFFERENT COUNTRIES (AS ON PAGE **72**) ARE USUALLY MADE USING **PURCHASING POWER PARITY (PPP)** EXCHANGE RATES, WHICH ARE BASED ON THE COST OF LIVING IN DIFFERENT COUNTRIES.

F

FEDERAL RESERVE ("THE FED")
THE CENTRAL BANK OF THE UNITED STATES: **37**
- AND GREAT DEPRESSION / GREAT RECESSION: **158–159**

FINANCIAL CRISIS

A BREAKDOWN IN THE BANKING SYSTEM: **163**

FISCAL POLICY

GOVERNMENT POLICIES RELATING TO TAXES AND SPENDING: **76–79**
- AND GREAT DEPRESSION: **160–161**
- CONTRAST WITH MONETARY POLICY: **76**

FREE-MARKET ECONOMICS

THE IDEA THAT ECONOMIC ACTIVITY SHOULD BE GUIDED BY THE "INVISIBLE HAND" WITHOUT GOVERNMENT INTERFERENCE: **11, 19, 164, 183**

G

GROSS DOMESTIC PRODUCT (GDP)

A MEASURE OF THE ECONOMIC POWER OF A COUNTRY OR OTHER REGION: **59–72**
- AND THE SIZE OF GOVERNMENT: **77, 84, 196–199**
- AND GOVERNMENT SPENDING ON FARMS AND FOREIGN AID: **138**
- DECLINE IN REAL GDP IN GREAT DEPRESSION AND GREAT RECESSION: **157**
- PER-CAPITA GDP AND CATCH-UP: **168–169**
- AND CLIMATE CHANGE: **191**

GDP DEFLATOR

A WAY TO MEASURE INFLATION THAT MACROECONOMISTS GENERALLY USE INSTEAD OF THE CPI BECAUSE IT FOCUSES ON **PRODUCTION** RATHER THAN **CONSUMPTION**: **66**

THE GDP DEFLATOR COMPARES PRICES IN YEARS X AND Y BY FIRST CALCULATING **NOMINAL GDP IN YEAR Y** (USING PRICES FROM YEAR Y), THEN CALCULATING **REAL GDP IN YEAR Y** (USING PRICES FROM YEAR X), AND THEN COMPARING THE TWO CALCULATIONS. HERE'S AN EXAMPLE:

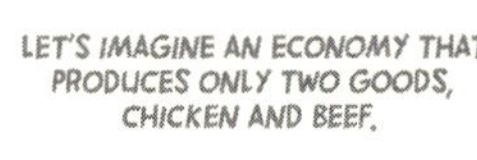

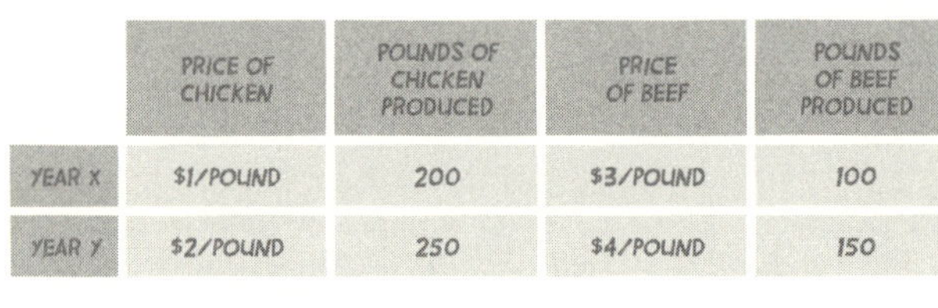

	PRICE OF CHICKEN	POUNDS OF CHICKEN PRODUCED	PRICE OF BEEF	POUNDS OF BEEF PRODUCED
YEAR X	$1/POUND	200	$3/POUND	100
YEAR Y	$2/POUND	250	$4/POUND	150

FIRST WE CALCULATE **NOMINAL GDP IN YEAR Y:**

$$(\$2 \times 250) + (\$4 \times 150) = \$1100$$

THEN WE CALCULATE **REAL GDP IN YEAR Y** USING **PRICES FROM YEAR X:**

$$(\$1 \times 250) + (\$3 \times 150) = \$700$$

FINALLY, WE CONCLUDE THAT INFLATION (AS MEASURED BY THE GDP DEFLATOR) WAS **57%** BETWEEN YEAR X AND YEAR Y BY COMPARING THE TWO:

$$\frac{\$1,100}{\$700} - 1 = 0.57$$

GOLD STANDARD

A MONETARY SYSTEM BASED ON THE VALUE OF GOLD: **215**

GREAT DEPRESSION

THE CATASTROPHIC ECONOMIC SLUMP THAT STARTED IN 1929: **10, 18, 155–166**
- AND "GREAT VACATION": **29**
- AND DEFLATION: **55**
- COMPARED TO "GREAT RECESSION" OF 2007–2009: **157**

"GREAT RECESSION" OF 2007–2009

THE WORST ECONOMIC DOWNTOWN IN THE U.S. SINCE THE GREAT DEPRESSION: **18, 70, 155**
- COMPARED TO GREAT DEPRESSION: **157**
- MONETARY AND FISCAL POLICY RESPONSE: **159–161**

INFANT INDUSTRY

THE ARGUMENT THAT TARIFFS OR OTHER TRADE BARRIERS SHOULD BE USED TO PROTECT SMALL DOMESTIC FIRMS FROM COMPETITION FROM BIG FOREIGN FIRMS: **113, 123**

INFLATION

A GENERAL INCREASE IN PRICES OVER TIME, OFTEN MEASURED WITH THE CPI OR THE GDP DEFLATOR: **44–58**
- ADJUSTMENTS IN SOCIAL SECURITY: **196**
- AND MONETARY POLICY: **48, 135, 215**
- AND REAL GDP: **65–68**
- SIMILARITIES WITH EXCHANGE RATE FLUCTUATIONS: **143**
- AND CURRENCY UNIONS: **146–147**
- AND INTEREST RATES: **52–53**

INTEREST RATE

THE RATE A BANK CHARGES YOU TO BORROW MONEY, OR THE RATE A BANK PAYS YOU TO SAVE MONEY: **41–44**
- AND MICROFINANCE: **132**
- AND ZERO LOWER BOUND: **159**
- NOMINAL VERSUS REAL INTEREST RATES: **52–53**

THE **RULE OF THUMB** RELATING THE NOMINAL INTEREST RATE (r_N), THE REAL INTEREST RATE (r_R), AND THE RATE OF INFLATION (i) IS:

$$r_R \approx r_N - i$$

FOR EXAMPLE, IF THE NOMINAL INTEREST RATE IS 6% ($r_N = 0.06$) AND THE RATE OF INFLATION IS 4% ($i = 0.04$) THE REAL INTEREST RATE IS ABOUT 2% ($r_R \approx 0.06 - 0.04 = 0.02$).

AS LONG AS INFLATION IS NOT TOO HIGH, THIS RULE OF THUMB IS A GOOD APPROXIMATION FOR THE **ACTUAL FORMULA**, WHICH IS:

$$r_R = \frac{1 + r_N}{1 + i} - 1$$

FOR $r_N = 0.06$ AND $i = 0.04$ WE GET $r_R = (1.06)/(1.04) - 1 = 0.019$.

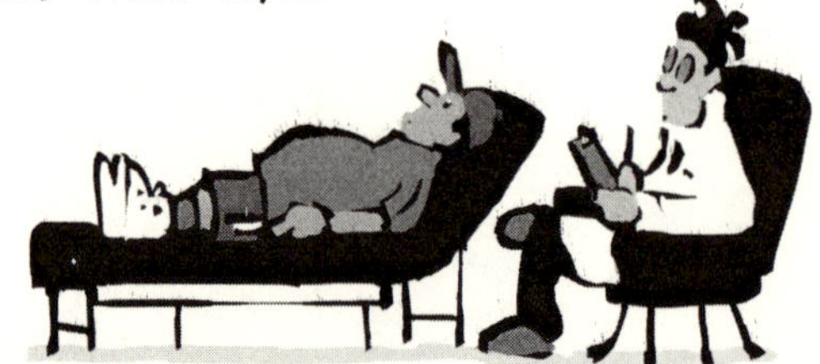

MORAL HAZARD
A SITUATION IN WHICH INSURANCE OR BAILOUTS END UP ENCOURAGING RISKY BEHAVIOR: **165**

N

NEOCLASSICAL SYNTHESIS
THE IDEA THAT MACROECONOMIES ARE KEYNESIAN IN THE SHORT RUN BUT CLASSICAL IN THE LONG RUN: **212**

NEUTRALITY OF MONEY
THE IDEA THAT A CHANGE IN THE VALUE OF MONEY—FOR EXAMPLE, A ONE-TIME OCCURRENCE OF 10% INFLATION—WILL NOT AFFECT REAL VARIABLES SUCH AS UNEMPLOYMENT: **34–37**
AND WHY INFLATION MATTERS: **48–49**

BECAUSE IT MAKES FOR FUN DRAWINGS, THIS BOOK ALSO USES (OR, MORE CORRECTLY, MISUSES) THE TERM **SUPER-NEUTRAL**, WHICH IS THE IDEA THAT CHANGES IN THE RATE OF GROWTH OF MONEY—FOR EXAMPLE, MOVING FROM 5% TO 10% INFLATION—WILL NOT AFFECT REAL VARIABLES.

NOMINAL VARIABLES
WAGES, PRICES, INTEREST RATES, OR OTHER VARIABLES THAT—IN CONTRAST TO REAL VARIABLES—CAN BE DISTORTED BY INFLATION, USUALLY BECAUSE THEY ARE EXPRESSED IN DOLLAR TERMS: **49–53**

O

OPEN-MARKET OPERATIONS
PURCHASES OR SALES OF GOVERNMENT BONDS OR OTHER ASSETS BY CENTRAL BANKS IN ORDER TO CHANGE THE MONEY SUPPLY: **40–43**

P

PARETO
THREE TERMS NAMED AFTER ITALIAN ECONOMIST VILFREDO PARETO. ONE OUTCOME IS A **PARETO IMPROVEMENT** OVER ANOTHER IF SWITCHING MAKES AT LEAST ONE PERSON BETTER OFF AND MAKES NOBODY WORSE OFF. ANY PARTICULAR OUTCOME IS EITHER **PARETO INEFFICIENT** OR **PARETO EFFICIENT** DEPENDING ON WHETHER THERE IS OR IS NOT ANY PARETO IMPROVEMENT OVER IT, I. E., ON WHETHER THERE IS OR IS NOT ANOTHER OUTCOME THAT MAKES AT LEAST ONE PERSON BETTER OFF WITHOUT MAKING ANYBODY WORSE OFF: **81, 93, 95, 98, 114**

PEAK COAL, PEAK OIL, ETC.
CONCERNS ABOUT RUNNING OUT OF RESOURCES SUCH AS OIL AND COAL: **181–185**

POVERTY TRAP
A SELF-REINFORCING CYCLE (INSTABILITY, WAR, LOW INVESTMENT, ETC.) THAT KEEPS POOR COUNTRIES TRAPPED IN POVERTY: **172–173**